Davide Frezzato

Control booth
Vision on Caravaggio

Proscenium

One more book about Caravaggio?
They wrote so much about him, is not it enough?

We might agree and state that they said even too much!

Today Caravaggio is one of the most loved artists on the Italian cultural scene and he plays the role of one of the main characters in national and popular culture. Yet in his life as an artist (much longer than that of a human being) he had to endure even the difficult moment of oblivion.
Being here to speak once again of his Art has great value. Michelangelo Merisi has created works so rich and full of meanings that we cannot afford the luxury of circumscribing it in an artistic movement nor can his works find a single interpretation. Much has been said based on biographical preconceptions and not silently observing his works. Caravaggio speaks to us, sometimes with a faint whisper, and tells us about himself in everything he has done.
In these pages I would like to accompany you to discover the show staged by Merisi; for this reason, I will avoid talking about interpretations and works about which they have already said and written, perhaps, too much. The excellent work of historians and critics who have offered their guidance in the knowledge and understanding of his canvases, however,

sometimes needs a little tumble turn. The myth of Caravaggio has to be revised, considering the fact that more than a painter he was a highly talented theatre director, who immortalized on his canvases the effort of actors (sometimes amateur) engaged in reciting historical and religious roles.

This is the reason why I thought of writing this book respecting the theatrical terminology, as if it were a script. Only by approaching his works with the expectation of the audience at theatres can we fully appreciate some of his compositional choices and we can better understand some keys of interpretation that can easily remain hidden among the brushstrokes of the Lombard master.

On some aspects of his Art I will essentially disagree with what has been said so far and sometimes I will take diametrically opposed positions with respect to the usual interpretation of his works. The dialectical debate, even violent but never rude, is necessary so that we can continue to create and let new life flow into Art and to offer those contrasting forces that lead to the creation of unique works.

I think the time has come to get comfortable in our slightly narrow armchair covered in dark red velvet, turn off the mobile phone and remember to snore softly: the curtain is rising, the show begins.

Good vision to all from the control booth.

ACT ONE

Scene I:
Ladies and gentlemen, the director

Find an agreement between those who consider the knowledge of an artist's private life as a priority in order to understand his Art and who says that artistic and private life must be divided and one should never influence the considerations that can be had on his artistic work is an almost impossible. The experts in History and Criticism of Art are divided on the matter.

Sometimes it seems possible to find an agreement between the two factions, while some other times it seems an unrealistic utopia. Among the pages of this book we will see how it is necessary to adopt both criteria, obviously based on the cases that will arise from time to time.

The first act of this show features the presentation of Caravaggio, a man who made painting the centre of his existence.

The word "show" will often occur in the pages of this book; it is one of the keys to interpretation that can reveal the artistic world of Caravaggio.

It is not easy to embark on a new path linked to the knowledge and interpretation of an artist's works. The effort we are asked to do is to get out of the well-established schemes of critical literature in order not to look too much to the past but to project ourselves forward!

Let me use a mountaineer image, we have to get off the track and follow a new one, a little more difficult and demanding but which will offer us a spectacular view of the artistic panorama of Caravaggio.

But let us get to the key: "show".

It is at the origins of the word theatre. Once again, to better enter the topic we need to come back to ancient Greek: θέατρον (théatron), which means "show". An aspect that cannot be overlooked is that we also find the same root in the Greek verb θεάομαι (theàomai), which means "to see".

These two words are the most concise and truthful description of the whole work by Caravaggio. His Art is, in all respects, a show and his personal vision of reality and the salient themes of life.

If we began to observe Caravaggio's works through the filter of these interpretations, many apparently incomprehensible aspects of his works would become understandable.

That is why we have to try to observe his canvases with a different sensitivity from what we are used to.

To do all this, let's not hide it, an act of courage is required. Questioning most of past studies can be uncomfortable. However, if we think about it, human evolution progresses by always questioning and creating discomfort.

Why should not we try?

On the other hand, we do not know what to expect, we could go down a dead end or maybe not. In both cases, there will be surprises, this is little but sure.

Scene II:
The mystery of a name

Before starting to speak freely of Michelangelo Merisi, we have to clarify an important aspect related to his name. For most, even among literate or alleged men, the reasons that led him to choose his stage name remain unclear: Caravaggio.

In Art only the greatest ones can afford the honour of being remembered with their first name. If we think of the finer minds of the Italian intellectual panorama we cannot forget Leonardo, Dante, Michelangelo and the first great recommended in the History of Art which was Raphael (sorry if I dropped a thrust against poor Raphael in this way, maybe I will have a way in other places to explain myself more profusely).

All these great artists are universally known by the first name only, since they are the worthiest of importance to have brought that name in the history of humanity.

Poor Michelangelo Merisi had to bear the same name of that Michelangelo Buonarroti who for all of us is, more simply, Michelangelo. Unquestionably, the figure of Michelangelo is a keystone in not only Italian but European artistic development. Faced with so much importance and uniqueness, his Lombard namesake could only opt for a stage name, since not only would it have been impossible to overcome the importance of the Florentine master but it would have been unlikely (and so it was) to match his size.

Thus, the choice fell on a small village near Bergamo: Caravaggio, in fact.

And so, it was that the problems due to an infinite series of mistakes based on a great inaccuracy began, errors that continued until Vittorio Pirami (ex Fininvest executive) during an amateur research on the painters who worked in the city of Milan gave space to the truth. In his research at the Diocesan Archive, Pirami comes across a document kept in such a very bad condition that in order to read it he is forced to use a Wood lamp; better known as UV lamp (exactly the one that is used in films to detect organic traces at the scene of a crime).

After the adventurous reading of this document, an uncomfortable information was discovered, immediately opposed by those who represent the town near Bergamo, which made the painter a real typical product.

The document attest, in fact, the birth of Michelangelo Merisi in the parish of Santo Stefano in Milan, baptized in the Milanese church of Santo Stefano in Brolo on 30th September 1571. This document is certainly not like a thunderbolt; already the well-known Roberto Longhi (important Art historian born in Alba in 1890 and died in Florence in 1970) had in fact speculated that Michelangelo Merisi was not born in the Bergamo area of Caravaggio but was a native of the Lombard capital. For Longhi the name could also be significant to reconstruct the date of birth of the little Michelangelo, probably come to light on 29th September on the occasion of the anniversary of St. Michael the Archangel.

The text of the document reads:

«*Adi 30 fu batz.o [battezzato] Michel angelo f[ilio] de d[omino] Fermo Merixio et d[omina] Lutia de Oratoribus/ compare d[omino] Fran[cesco] Sessa*».[1]

Everything would seem to coincide but, obviously, in the country of Caravaggio not everyone agrees. The mayor Ettore Pirovano at the time of the publication of the document, disputes the data saying that Michelangelo Merisi has always claimed to be a native of Caravaggio. As if the words of an artist were worth as much as a document. It is known that the

---

[1] The document was written in 16th century Italian. The translation of the text is: "Today Michel angelo was baptized son of Mr. Fermo Merixio and Lady Lutia de Oratoribus / fellow Mr. Francesco Sessa

biography of an artist (often also the autobiography) is elaborated for necessity or pure pleasure; all those who put themselves on the defensive cannot fail to consider a possible need of Caravaggio to "change" his personal history.

What remains undisputed is a universally recognized document preserved in the dubious hometown: the parental marriage certificate. Both parents were born in Caravaggio and were part of the high society. We should not forget that their wedding witness was the Marquis of Caravaggio and Count of Galliate: Francesco I Sforza. One wonders if the affection for the family of origin (or the possibility of being able to take advantage of a facilitated condition given by the parents' social background) led him to make the same choice as another illustrious Lombard: the lesser known Pietro Martire d'Anghiera. Historian who first wrote a report on the New World and committed himself to the use of corn all across our Continent. Born in Arona, on the Piedmont side of Lake Maggiore, he decided to be recognized as originally from Angera, a city on the Lombard side, in honour of his parents' origins. A better-known case is that of Carlo Lorenzini who chose the name of his mother's hometown to sign one of the world's best-known literary works: Pinocchio, signed as Carlo Collodi.

I believe that the inhabitants of the village so fond of Caravaggio (for obvious reasons) should accept this possibility, which more than anything else is a certainty.

You will notice that often I will take the liberty to turn to Caravaggio with his first name given the deep friendship that binds me to him after so many years spent in his pleasant company.

Dedicating yourself to the study of an artist means talking to him, discussing (sometimes even very animatedly) his choices, arguing and sitting at a table to have a drink together like old friends.

Those who create a work of Art manage to overcome the barrier of time and space and are always present alongside their work. With Michelangelo the chats are always many, outnumbered only by the pleasant quarrels in friendship, which have always been resolved with a toast to our respective health.

I strongly believe in this approach towards Art and artists; a work of Art is not a reminder of the technique or artistic depth of a great who has now passed away but a dialogue between living people, between alive and well sensitiveness.

A promise: if I have to call Michelangelo, Buonarroti, it will be my concern to appoint him properly, so as not to create unnecessary confusion.

Scene III:
An artist with a strong character

The training of an artist, considering studies and first work experiences, is essential to read his works. Obviously, the family context in which the future artist takes his first steps is also important, the real ones and not necessarily the artistic ones.

We have already seen in the previous scene that the Caravaggio family could count on many politically influential backers. The data relating to the habits and daily life of the Merisi family are not many, unfortunately; some of the information in our possession is reconstructed and others, even, are conjectures of historians and researchers.

What is certain, however, is that Michelangelo's father moved to Milan for work and brought his wife with whom he had married on 14th January 1571. The move to the big city was due to the fact, most likely, that the couple's wedding witness/protector had managed to find an employment for Fermo (this was the name of Caravaggio's father) in the *Fabbrica del Duomo*[2]. In the same month in which the wedding was celebrated the painter was conceived and he will become the pride (even if opposed in life) of Lombard and Italian painting; these are the biographical events that made the baby born in Milan.

Unfortunately, another certain fact is the role played by illness in Caravaggio's life.

The plague of Milan will make him fatherless. Curiously, this scourge that for centuries afflicted Europe also became the element that binds three of the most influential figures of Lombard culture: Caravaggio, Manzoni and Cardinal Federico Borromeo.

In 1577 the family of Fermo da Caravaggio returned to the country of origin in order to escape from the plague that had taken control of the Lombard capital. However, his father contracted the disease and died in a short time, together with his grandfather Bernardino and uncle Pietro. The epidemic did not fade quickly and lasted for about 13 years.

---

[2] By this name we mean all the workers employed in the construction of the imposing Milan Cathedral.

As soon as possible, the young Michelangelo returned to Milan and started working in Simone Peterzano's workshop.

He was a mannerist painter active in the time of the Counter-Reformation. The artistic style of the master of the workshop and this historical moment are extremely important in the formation of Caravaggio because they will strongly influence his way of Painting.

Mannerism is the pure theatricality of Painting. Worthy descendant of the exuberance of the Baroque, it gives human figures an exaggeration of feelings. The amazement, the pain and the joy are accentuated giving an almost caricatural impression. A bit like good theatre actors engaged in a sometimes very heavy effort to ensure that even the audience at the back of the room is joined by mimicry and theatrical expression; an aspect that is changing in contemporary theatre where the naturalness of acting is preferred.

As we will see, the aspect of theatricality is so strong in Caravaggio's Art that it can almost be called the Theatre himself.

The Counter-Reformation, born mainly as a political response to a religious need, represented a turning point in customs and culture. From the crackdown of Saint Charles Borromeo towards the somewhat too libertine habits of the clergy to the excessive use of colour, the Counter-Reformation represented an abysmal change. A change that led, among other things, to the birth of what will be Caravaggio's true signature: black colour.

In Peterzano's workshop, Caravaggio breathed these ideas and his Art was formed on them. Even around the figure of the master of the shop the information is not always certain; he himself signed in some works such as Titian's master. A nice attempt to give himself more importance than he perhaps deserved and it is curious to think that at that moment he was the master of a future great name of Italian Art and did not know it.

The school at Peterzano lasted four years. In his master's workshop, Caravaggio learned the lesson of the great artists of the Lombard and Venetian schools very well; lessons that he would soon change with his personal style.

Interesting is what Giulio Mancini, one of Caravaggio's biographers who lived between 1558 and 1630, writes:

> «*Studiò in fanciullezza per quattro o cinque anni in Milano, con diligenza ancorché di quando in quando facesse qualche stravaganza causata da quel calore e spirito così grande*».[3]

From a young age, Caravaggio's character was difficult to manage, both because of his short-tempered and animated side and for his innovative spirit and not very suitable to follow academic rules. Many of his works should be read in view of his strong personality; this is the only way to understand some rash and decidedly unorthodox choices.

The contract that his mother signed with Peterzano ended in 1588. Until 1592 Caravaggio remained in Lombardy but we

---

[3] He studied in childhood for four or five years in Milan, with diligence even if from time to time he did some extravagance caused by that so great warmth and spirit.

do not have sufficient documentation to be able to reconstruct its activities in these years. Based on the reconstruction of Giulio Mancini, Caravaggio's mother died in Milan on 29th November 1590; the date can be calculated thanks to the documents relating to the division of the woman's inheritance.

In the middle of 1592 Caravaggio left Lombardy and went to Rome. According to the documents kept in the State Archives of Rome we know that until 1496, Caravaggio was a very restless man. He was unable to remain on a permanent basis in the Eternal City but continued to move.

Much more fascinating is the theory of Giovan Pietro Bellori (Art historian and writer born and lived in Rome between 1613 and 1696). In his works the young Merisi is described as a young painter

«*d'ingegno torbido e contentioso*»[4].

Due to not well defined

«*discordie*»[5]

---

[4] The text is written in ancient Italian: "with turbid and contentious genius".

[5] The Italian text says: "discords".

it seems that Caravaggio had to leave Milan and that he arrived

«*in Venetia ove si compiacque tanto del colorito di Giorgione, che se lo propose per iscorta nell'imitatione*»[6].

Bellori also speaks of Venice in his biography. However, he states that the trip has been done together with Peterzano and that it was very short. This version of events is still highly debated among Art historians because unfortunately it is not supported by any type of document.

Undoubtedly the Art of Caravaggio owes a lot to the Venetian School; his style is strongly linked to that of Giorgione, Titian and Tintoretto. The fact that Merisi could know this artistic sensitivity in depth is also historically explainable: the geographical boundaries of the Most Serene Republic of Venice reached as far as Bergamo.

Roberto Longhi also attributes a strong influence in the Art of Caravaggio to the Lombard masters - especially those in the area of Brescia- among the most important names he cites Foppa, Bergognone, Savoldo, Moretto and Romanino.

Although scarce, the data on Caravaggio's training offer us an important reading key to observe his beautiful works with a sometimes-disturbing force.

---

[6] The text is written in old Italian: "in Venice where he was so pleased with Giorgione's color, that he proposed it for an idea to imitate".

Caravaggio faces high-calibre names with regards to the Venetian School, which in this period has reached a very high artistic level. At the same time, Lombardy is a land that receives influences from abroad (Florence was the capital of a foreign state at the time, let's not forget it) and it is an interesting crossroads where it seems difficult to get noticed. Caravaggio's restlessness will lead him to move to be able to dare more and more, to become someone.

His paintings are never too faithful to the subject represented; they are to be seen and read as an inner image of the mind and personality of Caravaggio and his world, made of worldliness and limits to overcome, even going against the peaceful common sense.

There is no brush stroke by Caravaggio that cannot be read as a hymn to ecstasy. Everything is tension and life, blood and corporeality. Everything in his Art tells us about the perpetual internal struggle that animates the spirit of Caravaggio since his tender age.

Not a madman, not a violent one (as too many historians have described it for ease) but a restless person who cannot accept the rules of the academy without contesting them; an artist who cannot accept dogmas because they block human ability to understand and represent.

This strong character animates Caravaggio's works that, perhaps more than anyone else, has managed to instil life in Art.

His own life and view of the world.

Scene IV:
On the edge of the centre of society

Usually we are led to associate the figure of Caravaggio with smoky and gloomy taverns, frequented by people who lived on the edge of society.

This does not stray far from reality. Caravaggio loved to frequent that world, and he also used it as scenography for many of his scenes, even religious ones.

He can be considered the typical profile for a probable murderer, a violent, prostitute-goer and friend of criminals. In a nutshell, an outcast of society who among stab wounds found time to paint too.

Caravaggio was exactly like this?

I do not think so. Or rather, not completely.

Undoubtedly, Caravaggio had a very strong and irascible temper, which resulted in episodes of violence. This can also be seen from his handwriting, which was analysed by Dr. Evi Crotti, confirming what we already knew.

In addition to his inability to manage anger, interesting details have emerged. According to the study of Dr. Crotti, the particular conformation of the capital "M" and the connection in the couple of letters "ch", in addition to the presence of angular letters, denote a certain ostentation and also a marked creativity. Of a certain importance is the fluidity of his stroke (despite the many stains he left on the paper) which highlights his tendency not to be able to wait; a personality perpetually accompanied by anxiety.

A person with a similar character is not an easy company and for this reason they kept him as far as possible from the sumptuous courts, which were quietly frequented by characters such as Raphael and where even Michelangelo Buonarroti was not very comfortable.

Yet Caravaggio also frequented the "good society" of the Italian capital and beyond.

In particular, he was a friend of Cardinal Francesco Maria del Monte whom he had known in 1597 and became a real guardian angel for Caravaggio. In addition to having bought him some paintings - among which also the famous cheaters - he also did much more: he took him to work at his home for about three years.

Even according to Bellori, Cardinal del Monte is partly responsible for his social and artistic rise, in fact he

«ridusse in buono stato Michele e lo sollevò dandogli luogo onorato in casa fra i gentiluomini»[7].

It is thanks to this influential friendship that Caravaggio is at the centre of the salons of the high Roman nobility.

This social climb is easy to see even in his painted canvases. In fact, at the beginning, we did not have large canvases and his pictorial style was mainly aimed at creating small portraits - not full-length, of course - and the themes were quite simple.

Now, thanks to the commissions of his influential protector, the canvases become much larger and the painted themes are increasingly complex. The canvases are crowded with an increasing number of characters - the painting "Rest on the Flight into Egypt", so to speak, it was made in this period - and they no longer offer an immediate and simplified reading. All this made his fame grow exponentially until he even became a living myth.

Caravaggio, as we will also see in some of his works, was an eccentric and despite the new social status achieved, he continued to hang out in the low funds. But we cannot bind it only in the taverns in our imagination.

---

[7] The document is written in old Italian: "he transformed Michele into good condition and raised him, giving him an honoured place in the house among the gentlemen"

Influential friendships have never been lacking in Caravaggio's life. Let us not forget that despite his troubles with the law, Michelangelo was helped by the nobility and the powerful order of the Knights of Malta to escape the harsh sentence inflicted on him - mostly for political reasons - following the murder of Ranuccio Tommasoni from Terni: the beheading that could be executed by anyone who had even met him on the street.

Among his important friendships we have to remember the ambassador of France, who had taken him directly under his personal protection. This friendship was very dangerous for Caravaggio; in fact, when he killed Ranuccio - who belonged to a pro-Spanish family - his sentence was aggravated due to his proximity to the French area.

Due to the sentence, it was no longer possible for Caravaggio to live in the capital. So, he decided to run away, not an easy task but with the right friendships it was not impossible, obviously.

Thanks to the help of Prince Philip I Colonna (one of the most powerful and important families in Italy), Caravaggio manages to find refuge and hide. In fact, the prince hosted him in one of his Roman fiefdoms - the territory under his dominion expanded between Marino, Palestrina, Zagarolo and Paliano.

Caravaggio's escape was a perfect orchestration between several members of the Colonna family - all directed by Filippo I - who testified the forgery by signalling the presence of Caravaggio in the city where he had never been. In a short time, his traces were lost, thus allowing him to reach the Spanish quarters of Naples, the city where a branch of the Colonna family resided: the Carafa-Colonna.

In the Neapolitan city Caravaggio lives a very happy period, despite the death penalty hanging over his head. During this period, he worked a lot and one of his canvases also arrived in Flanders.

Always thanks to the intercession of the powerful Colonna, Caravaggio manages to reach Malta where he not only gets in touch with the prestigious order of the Knights of Malta but will also become a novice and will be awarded the title of "knight of grace", title that could be obtained after a year of novitiate. To then be mysteriously put into prison and consequently removed.

Was it possible that the powerful order knew nothing of his death sentence? It is a little difficult to believe.

The truth could hide itself - once again - behind its bad character. It seems, in fact, that Caravaggio quarrelled very hard with a knight of superior rank and consequently they expelled him with dishonour.

It is likely that the dispute did not erupt following the discovery of Caravaggio's past misdeeds and his death sentence. Envy, jealousy or resentment could have led the two to quarrel and a consequent social pillory, which obviously has once again fallen on the one who has always shown his indomitable and violent side.

Among various vicissitudes, Caravaggio arrives in Sicily where he finds refuge at the home of Mario Minniti, a long-time friend of his and also a painter. Obviously, the important commissions - even from the Dorias - are not long in coming.

The return to Naples is almost an obligation, since with the Colonna family he has a difficult debt to pay and the marquise Costanza opens the doors of her palace in Cellammare for him.

Caravaggio's contacts allow him to get to the Pope - we should not forget that the Colonna will also come to play the role of successors of Saint Peter - to ask for the papal amnesty of the sentence.

On the other hand, we know it very well, Italy is indeed the home of saints, thieves and navigators... but also of amnesties of all kinds.

And freedom obviously has a price, which Caravaggio negotiates with Cardinal Scipione Borghese: paintings (obviously). As in the best sagas, the cargo is lost and those who offer to give Caravaggio a boat to be able to recover it is the family Orsini, one of the oldest princely and papal families in Rome.

Finally, after such a gruelling diplomacy and pleasure shopping, everything is ready. Once the offering has been paid, papal grace will come.

And the unexpected happens.

Death will knock on the door of the most irascible and diplomatic man who can be known and will frustrate everything.

It is clear that we cannot continue to think of Caravaggio as an outcast frequenting taverns and prostitutes. All these contacts, all these favours obviously presuppose an infinite series of exchanges of favours and gifts - mainly works of Art - but also a certain attendance. Let us not forget that too often we forget that Caravaggio's origins are not exactly humble and "normal".

A nobleman over the top. That was our Caravaggio.

Scene V:
A long trail of violence

That our Caravaggio was very far from being an angel, we certainly do not need to remember it.

It is curious, to tell the truth, to see what the condition of our painter's criminal record really was.

I can tell you that among minor and more serious crimes, his situation would envy a crime professional, even if we don't know much about his brutal adventures in Milan. We have seen in the previous chapters that from his young age he showed a character that warmed up very easily. Reliable or not, Bellori's considerations do not seem so abstruse, according to which he certainly made himself known in Milan for his lack of mildness.

With the arrival in Rome, in an environment unrelated to the Milanese protectorate partly guaranteed by his surname, Caravaggio did not take long to build a reputation among the violent ones.

The first episode takes place in the prestigious home of Cardinal Del Monte on 28th November 1600. Here was also a noble prelate, a guest of the cardinal, whose name was Girolamo Stampa from Montepulciano (an amazing little town in Tuscany), who was literally beaten by Caravaggio. We do not know exactly what triggered this violent quarrel between the two; it is certain that we do not have much difficulty imagining our dear Caravaggio in a similar situation. Obviously, the noble beaten prelate denounced the painter.

In the prisons of Tor di Nona, the presence of Caravaggio was considered normal. Due to multiple charges he was often arrested and brought here in handcuffs; among the causes were an increasing number of complaints about fights, violence and disturbances.

All in all, he was an accursed artist *ante litteram*, he lacked only the famous absinthe and would have been perfect sitting at a 19th century Parisian bar.

A few months later - in 1601 - he left prison and devoted himself a little more calmly to painting.

Although the problems with the law did not take long to return.

In 1603, in fact, he was again sentenced. This time the offense was defamation. Giovanni Baglione - a Roman painter born in 1573 and died in 1643 - did not like at all some rhymes that Caravaggio had written in the company of his fellows Orazio Gentileschi - a little likeable father of the most famous Artemisia - and Onorio Longhi.

At the State Archives of Rome are kept not only the seized documents inherent to the lawsuit but also the testimonies of the three painters who were sued by poor Baglione; a painter who, let us face it, is remembered mostly for the lawsuit and not so much for his Art.

As we will see, the rhymes written by the three artists are decidedly goliardic, almost like university students who lash out against a poor freshman.

The magistrate, during the process, collects the deposition of Caravaggio, which in some moments is a real disquisition related to his idea of Art:

«*Quella parola, valent'huomo, appresso di me vuol dire che sappi far bene, cioè sappi far bene dell'arte sua, così un pittore valent'huomo, che sappi depinger bene et imitar bene le cose naturali*»[8].

Furthermore, his criticisms of those whom he cannot define painters are also collected in the documents:

---

[8] "That word, talented man, for me means that you know how to do well, that is, you know how to do well of your art, so a talented painter, who knows how to paint well and imitate natural things well"

> «Li valent'huomini sono quelli che si intendono della pittura et giudicaranno buoni pittori quelli che ho giudicato io buoni et cattivi; ma quelli che sono cattivi pittori et ignoranti giudicaranno per buoni pittori gl'ignoranti come sono loro»[9].

Let us now return to the two incriminated texts:

> «Gioan Bagaglia tu non sai un ah
> le tue pitture sono pituresse
> volo vedere con esse
> che non guadagnarai
> mai una patacca
> che di cotanto panno
> da farti un paro di bragesse
> che ad ognun mostrarai
> quel che fa la cacca
> porta là adunque
> i tuoi desegni e cartoni
> che tu ai fatto a Andrea pizicarolo
> veramente forbetene il culo
> alla moglie di Mao turegli la potta
> che [...] con quel suo cazzon
> da mulo più non la fotte

---

[9] "The talented men are those who understand of painting and those who will judge to be good and bad painters those who I have judged to be good or bad; but those who are bad and ignorant painters will judge the ignorant as good painters as they are"

perdonami dipintore se io non ti adulo
che della collana che tu porti indegno sei
et della pittura vituperio»[10].

The second, however, reads:

«Gian Coglion senza dubio dir si puole
quel che biasimar si mette altrui
che può cento anni esser mastro di lui.
Nella pittura intendo la mia prole
poi che pittor si vol chiamar colui
che non può star per macinar con lui.
I color non ha mastro nel numero
si sfaciatamente nominar si vole
si sa pur il proverbio che si dice
che chi lodar si vole si maledice.
Io non son uso lavarmi la bocca
né meno di inalzar quel che non merta
come fa l'idol suo che è cosa certa.
Se io mettermi volesse a ragionar
delle scaure fatte da questui
non bastarian interi un mese o dui.

---

[10] "Gioan Bagaglia you don't know an ah/your paintings are stupid little things/I want to see with them/that you won't earn/never a worthless coin/that of so much cloth/to make you a pair of pants/that you will show to each one/what poop does/bring there therefore/your drawings and cartoons/that you made for Andrea the Grocer/really clean your ass off/of Mao's wife fill her the slot/who [...] with that big cock of his/as the one of a mule he no longer fuck her/forgive me painter if I don't flatter you/that of the necklace you wear unworthy you are/and of painting you are reproach".

> *Vieni un po' qua tu ch'e vò' biasimare*
> *l'altrui pitture et sai pur che le tue*
> *si stano in casa tua a' chiodi ancora*
> *vergognandoti tu mostrarle fuora.*
> *Infatti i' vo' l'impresa abandonare*
> *che sento che mi abonda tal materia*
> *massime s'intrassi ne la catena*
> *d'oro che al collo indegnamente porta*
> *che credo certo meglio se io non erro*
> *a piè gle ne staria una di ferro.*
> *Di tutto quel che ha detto con passione*
> *per certo gli è perché credo beuto*
> *avesse certo come è suo doùto*
> *altrimente ei saria un becco fotuto.»*[11].

Goliardery has always existed, at all levels of society and at any cultural level. And as it often happens, it ends in defamation.

---

[11] Gian Asshole without a doubt can be said/who blames the others/who can be a hundred years a master of his./In painting I mean my offspring/then what pictorial he wanted to be called/who can't be about to grind with him./The colours has no master in the number/you bluntly nominate you want/the proverb that is said is known/that those who praise themselves want to curse themselves./I am not used to wash my mouth/no less than raising what does not deserve/as does his idol which is certain./If I wanted to reason/of the ugly things made by this one/one entire month or two will not be enough./Come here for a while you who want to blame/someone else's paintings and you know yours/they stay in your house on nails again/ashamed of showing them out./In fact, I want to abandon the enterprise/that I feel that subjects abounds me/at best if I could enter the chain/of gold that unworthily wears around the neck/which I certainly believe better if I'm not mistaken/at his feet it stands an iron one./Of everything he said with passion/for sure it is because I think he is drunk/had certain how his duty is/otherwise he will be a little screwed.

These colourful verses went around the city for several months, before Baglione, no longer enduring the situation, decided to report the three authors to the authorities; it is very likely that they were written mainly by Caravaggio and the other two were only secondary characters in this scene.

These early experiences of trials and incarcerations did not serve much for Caravaggio, who continued to live on the edge of legality, won by an increasingly intense flightiness.

In 1604 in a few months - between May and October - he was arrested several times. The charges were mainly for possession of weapons and for insults against city guards; one can easily understand that Caravaggio's spirit often went against the rules and those who respect them or must enforce them. This rebellion is an innate characteristic of his character and way of thinking, to the point that we will also find it in many of his works, both as regards civic and religious themes.

In 1604 he was sued again, this time by a boy from an inn where Caravaggio had gone to eat, he ordered a plate of artichokes - typical of the cuisine of Rome - which ended up in the face of the poor boy, because it was not to his taste.

In 1605 he even had to flee from Rome to take refuge in Genoa, obviously due to another problem with the law. This time he seriously injured nothing less than a notary, Mariano Pasqualone from Accumuli, because of a woman named Lena, who was a lover of Caravaggio. This case required the intervention of its Roman protectors who thanks to their influence managed to cover up the whole history and allowed Caravaggio to return to Rome.

Immediately after his return, he was sued again; this time it was his landlady, Ms. Prudenzia Bruni, for not having paid the rent. Caravaggio, out of spite, waited for the dark of the night to go and break the windows of poor Ms. Bruni's house with stones.

In November of the same year - always 1605 - there is a very curious fact in the biography of Caravaggio; the painter was hospitalized because of an injury caused by an accidental fall on the sword he carried on his waist. If we want, it's a highly suspicious case; especially if we consider his life so far. Apparently, the wound was inflicted on him during a hidden duel or in an ambush following a revenge.

On 28th May 1606 the most serious event was recorded in the biography of the Lombard painter. That evening Caravaggio started a game of royal tennis together with Ranuccio Tommasoni from Terni (a person that Merisi already knew and with whom he had already repeatedly fought violently). During this game Caravaggio suffered a foul committed by Ranuccio and the quarrel was not long in coming on; Ranuccio injured Caravaggio, who in turn wounded him mortally.

At the basis of this fight - set off by a banal foul - there seems to be much more; the two loved the same woman, Fillide Melandroni, who gave all her attentions to both men. It even seems that this situation may have erupted due to an unpaid debt; the two had a lot of fun playing and betting and Caravaggio paid his debts with great difficulty. We cannot even ignore the political aspect of the situation. Ranuccio's family was notoriously pro-Spanish, while Caravaggio was protected by the French ambassador.

Considering all these different facets related to the death of Ranuccio Tommasoni, we can understand why the sentence imposed on Caravaggio was so heavy: beheading. With an aggravating circumstance against the painter, the sentence could be carried out by anyone who met Caravaggio, even if they had simply met him on the street.

These facts are important to know and not to give vent to a general and prevailing need for gossip but to understand the artistic choices of the great Lombard painter, who with his Art has influenced not only Italian culture.

Many artistic choices of Caravaggio find explanation in his strong character and in his innate tendency to be desecrator and provoker. Too often we wanted to find hidden messages or revolutionary ideas; I firmly believe that it is more correct to read his works by making constant reference to his biography and psychology.

Caravaggio seems to have never experienced an interest in religious messages and concepts, much less for the historical-social ones. The Lombard painter dedicated his life to the search for beauty, declined according to his personal language, not accepted from the beginning and also fallen into oblivion for some time. Another aspect to which he has always been faithful is that of fun, of teasing (even if it is irreverent) and potentially subject to lawsuit.

Scene VI:
A life on the run

As we have already seen, a constant in Caravaggio's life is represented by flight.

From an early childhood he found himself having to face the difficult experience of having to leave his home, move away from the environments of daily life and affections in order to rebuild his own world elsewhere.

Of many escapes experienced due to the plague or its violent character, it will be the one caused by Tommasoni's murder that will arouse greater sensitivity in his painting on the theme of death, as well as hitting our imagination more.

This impact so visible in his works originates in the daring escape plan organised thanks to the complicity of the Colonna family, which will take him to the island of Malta; a place that in addition to its natural charm due to the geographical conformation of an island also enjoyed the charm brought by the Knights of Malta, who kept close to the myth.

This continuous movement, this continuous lack of a reference point meant that Caravaggio did not feel in his Art a particular attachment for a teacher or for a school in particular. He, like Dante, learned the taste that reigned in Italy, lived for pleasure in the slums and for family extraction and economic interest could be found in the most beautiful residences of the Roman nobility. Italian culture and society belonged to him in a transversal way and he knew how to speak to the masses as the cultural elite of the time.

All this we can perceive also from his paintings, refined and pervaded by the smoke of the taverns. Even when he has to satisfy the requests of a commission, Caravaggio inserts personal aspects into his works, he always talks about himself and above all, a very important aspect of his way of conceiving Art: he enjoys himself.

The historical reconstructions in his paintings - especially in those with a religious background - are in themselves theatrical works born from the inventiveness of the painter who seems to want to create a world in his image and likeness, where he can finally feel comfortable and take root.

If we think about his life well, he has always created his own cohort or, by entering into existing cohorts, he has become the centre of interest in cultural life. From the gang of goliardic artists sued for the obscene and slanderous poems, to his enormous effort to enter the Order of the Knights of Malta, Caravaggio has always worked hard not to find himself alone. His Art finds inspiration and strength from friendship, it seems that he wants to escape solitude. His models were like actors in a company that had him as the actor-manager. From single portraits to group ones we notice that atmosphere of scenic stillness typical of those who posed, satisfying the requests of a rather demanding director.

If on the one hand we cannot fail to consider his paintings as real works of Art that open - even violently - the doors to an innovation unparalleled for the time, on the other we must - for intellectual honesty - consider the paintings by Caravaggio as an extreme attempt to create a world in which to find oneself, in which the painter could not only feel at home but could feel at ease.

From the study of light, used in a unique way and transformed into a feature so recognizable as to make Caravaggio's Art unmistakable - copied by painters of different eras and nationalities - to the theatricality of expressions and scenography - as we will see in some of his works - we are faced with a utopia, in which the painter wanted to live.

Caravaggio's works convey a strong intimacy, which seems to bind the artist and the models that wink and look intensely in the direction of the painter, a position that we now occupy as spectators. This intimacy is real, often Caravaggio asked friends or acquaintances to pose for the realization of his works. As said before, since when we look at his works we find ourselves taking the place of the painter, it seems to us that the protagonists look at us with that understanding that attracts us and makes us live special sensations and makes us love even more painting by Caravaggio.

There is no work by Caravaggio that does not create these sensations.

That's why all his works are easily recognizable and we don't even have to be particularly prepared to recognize his authorship.

Only one artist managed to create the same intimacy and intensity in her works, reaching the level of Caravaggio: Artemisia Gentileschi. A woman who preceded the times and who found in Caravaggio and his Art a very important and significant guide. To tell the truth, Artemisia seems to have been influenced by Michelangelo Merisi also in daily life; recent studies on this fabulous woman have shown that she loved attending taverns and did not mind participating in quarrels, small scuffles and took what and who she liked most without great problems.

Scene VII:
The theatrical direction

As we have already seen, a constant in Caravaggio's life is represented by flight. Caravaggio's painting is not only relegated to the field of Art impressed on canvases.

We should make our own the idea that his Art is also and above all theatre.

Each of his paintings is imbued with theatricality to the point that his scenes are occupied by real actors committed to giving life to their characters, following well-defined and studied canvases.

If we look at his *Bacchus* or *The Calling of St. Matthew* we perfectly realize how great is the importance that Caravaggio has always given to the theatre.

Several times I have reminded you that he was an assiduous inhabitant of taverns and nightlife, as well as a lover of all types of entertainment: among these we have not to forget to list the theatre.

We have to go back in time for a moment, making a small jump in one of the most interesting and culturally splendid eras: the Middle Ages. Let us think of the fabulous medieval bestiaries, which in addition to introducing us to the strangest beings that ever existed, offered us a whole series of information on the positive and negative qualities and habits of the human being. In these literary educational works, often, the fun linked to theatres was reported among the most sinful aspects of human life.

Let us not forget that our Milanese master was a lover of forbidden pleasure (or even frowned upon) and as a good provoker he never missed an opportunity to give scandal and to tie his image with depravity. The ideas and considerations born in the Middle Ages have survived for many centuries (some are still alive and well today) and the perception of the world of the Theatre was still in vogue at the time of Caravaggio, who obviously did not miss the opportunity to make it become a recurring theme in his Art and in his life.

In addition to being an excellent director, Michelangelo is an incredible set designer, screenwriter and lighting technician. Nothing seems to escape his attentive and alert eye. The composition of his works is always well studied and structured and the drama of the actors' expressions is expertly amplified and underlined by the effects of light.

The poses of the characters sometimes engage the actor-model so much, causing such physical as well as emotional tension, which also affects our senses, making us taking part to that effort and that swirl of emotions. It seems that the painter asked to exaggerate a movement or a cry and to prune the mimicry to excess so that they could be perceived even by those who were sitting in the back rows at the bottom of a theatre. The same commitment of having to amplify the feeling and expression is experienced by the artists on stage, who must impart such force to their actions as to reach even the most distant person in the audience. That feeling of extreme ecstasy as well as emotional discomfort that we perceive while looking at Caravaggio's paintings is due to the fact that his works are real amplifiers of emotions and feelings.

Silence in *The Calling of St. Matthew* is one of the main characters of the canvas. In our mind the whole scene is perfectly recreated, it is not difficult for us to imagine the characters of the story seated at the table intent on carrying out their profession, engaged in eagerly counting the coins collected for taxes, setting aside those for their own pockets.

Everything is built with a perfect theatrical rhythm (or if we want cinematic, why not).

The "bag guys" are engaged in animated goliardic discussions, waiting to intimidate some unfortunate payer called to pay their taxes.

A disciple of Jesus turns his back on us - very probably Peter himself - while he is intent on attracting the attention of those present, too busy in their chores to realize the newcomers.

Christ is calling to him the one who will become his new disciple.

All this would be perfect in some sweetened and well laid out film like the ones in Zeffirelli's style but it would not clash even in some scene full of pathos and strong tension like in a Mel Gibson's movie.

In spite of these sensations, those present give us anything but movement; they don't seem to come to life. The impression is almost that of being in front of a storyboard.

The characters are strictly static, as if they had been frozen by some still image.

In fact, Caravaggio does not seem to be possessed by the need to infuse life and movement into his works of art; as instead was Michelangelo of the History of Art (the one of David and the Sistine Chapel, to be clear). A real obsession that has turned into the legend according to which Buonarroti even went so far as to hammer his Moses by asking him eagerly:

Why do not you talk?

A beautiful story all there; I really struggle to believe that Buonarroti has made this gesture. He knows what is the right way to infuse life and movement to his sculptures; being the master of the *non finito*: his sculptural technique which is the best expedient to infuse real life and movement into the inorganic marble and the figures he sculpted in it.

The great innovators, the undisputed geniuses of Art like our two Michelangelo knew perfectly well that the only way to overcome the limits of Art was to take new paths and not continue to do things the old way, hoping to find some solution.

As for Caravaggio, we know that he will become the protagonist of many rumours, some will even become real legends, but none of these wants to lead us to think that the Lombard master had a real obsession to instil life in his works of art.

We know that one of Caravaggio's headshots was caused by his need to have the right light to paint. A light that many times was artificial, coming from candles, but often it was natural even if directed. This necessity led him to drill a hole in the roof of his residence-studio, which he had rented from poor Prudenzia Bruni (of which we have already spoken earlier). Thanks to this hole in the ceiling, the light entered the darkness of the studio illuminating the scene according to the needs of the painter-director. If we think about it, we are not so far from theatrical lighting with its directed light beams and ox-eyes.

There is no work by Caravaggio that does not present a sentient and collaborative light, which ends up being the main character of the works. All the other characters, even if they are in the main roles, are always secondary to the presence of this light that creates and shapes everything.

That Michelangelo Merisi is a director is a fact, not a reverie. Let us take some of his colleagues who are our contemporaries, regardless of the style and subjects commonly treated; there is not much difference among Caravaggio and Steven Spielberg, Francis Ford Coppola or Tim Burton (just to name a few). A director takes inspiration from his daily life and from his inner world to create his works; if we think of Tim Burton's films, we understand very well which world belongs to the director's imagination without even needing to listen to a single interview, which would confirm our suppositions.

Caravaggio is obsessed with darkness and light, finds a strong attraction for people who are different from the world in which he lives and is protected, so he takes refuge in the world of the night street and uses it as a corollary for all the scenes that he wants to represent, from myth to religion.

The aspect that we could define more cinematic and that is a characteristic of his way of painting is given by the camera obscura. We have already been told that Caravaggio painted looking at his models, his scenes and his still lives through a camera obscura, very similar to the modern camera. It does not take much imagination to see Caravaggio at work, in front of the canvas, while he observes the actors posing, with the lights well oriented on the scene, who observes everything from his camera obscura. If we think about it, however, it is not a scene very different from that of the director, sitting in front of the actors on stage, with the lights positioned in the right way and that after shouting "action" watches the scenes shot by the camera directly on the small screen through which he manages to get an idea of what the final result of the shooting will be.

Caravaggio should also be seen in this perspective. In no way would this lead to consider him a not so good painter. He is undoubtedly a painter with a talent that few before him have developed; that of painting a theatrical reality created on purpose with the sole purpose of creating a canvas.

Caravaggio is in all respects the screenwriter of his own stories narrated in painting. Furthermore, being a provoker, he loves to revisit the classics with a touch of modernity, which can sometimes vibrate like a dissonant note on a note sheet. So, his reinterpretations of the sacred and mythological scenes become at times desecrating but always extremely sincere, according to his personal vision and of those who think like him.

Caravaggio's Art has been widely copied and has also become a source of inspiration for painters of his own generation and for subsequent generations. Many have tried to copy his painting, not succeeding fully, precisely because they have tried to enclose his Art only and exclusively in Painting. So unfortunately, it was impoverished by the many *Caravaggisti* who have never managed to match the master's skill.

Among other things, Caravaggio's consideration of those who copied from the other painters is by no means flattering: he did not look favourably on the artists (whom he publicly disparaged) who merely copied from others and were not directly influenced by Nature.

It is a very important and curious aspect, for this we will have the opportunity to deepen it later. Caravaggio is still one of the most copied painters today, even by our contemporary artists: who knows how he would have treated him in seeing his works copied without restraint...

Scene VIII:
The dauber

An artist of the calibre of Caravaggio could not please everyone, obviously.

While today it seems that universally there is a strong love for his Art and that seems to be recognized as a cornerstone of the evolution of the History of Art, in the past - especially with the contemporaries - Caravaggio has had a fair amount of problems.

The first obstacle that Michelangelo Merisi had to overcome was that which all the artists had in common (and still share among them today): make themselves known.

Stopping in front of the *Basket of Fruit* kept at the Pinacoteca Ambrosiana in Milan, it is exciting to think that that canvas has travelled kilometres rolled up in the young painter's bag. This long pilgrimage will end in Rome, when the canvas will be given by Cardinal Del Monte to one of the eminences of the culture of the time, as well as his colleague: Cardinal Federico Borromeo.

Caravaggio's fame was a real media event for the time. Much honour and praise also brought envious detractors; a life as a "cursed artist" *ante litteram* in a highly respectable society caused him a lot of criticism and lastly, unfortunately, we must remember that his so innovative and unique Art was not very understood and consequently was strongly opposed.

One of the first strong criticisms received (and also the hardest to accept) was a free malice on the part of Giovanni Baglione (exactly the man of the libel trial).

Baglione tells us that the canvas representing *The Inspiration of Saint Matthew* was made in a first version, then rejected by the client (Francesco Contarelli), considering it not worthy of the family chapel. Thus, our Michelangelo Merisi had to make a new one which would be the one we can admire today in the famous chapel at the church of St. Louis of the French in Rome.

Studies carried out in 2000 by the Italian Art historian Luigi Spezzaferro would have shown that what told by Baglione would be a beautiful and good lie, created artfully to discredit the much-hated Caravaggio.

But Bellori also reports a similar episode, also involving Vincenzo Giustiniani, the protector of Caravaggio:

«*Qui avvenne cosa, che pose in grandissimo disturbo, e quasi fece disperare Caravaggio in riguardo della riputazione; poiché avendo egli terminato il quadro di mezzo di San Matteo e postolo sù l'altare, fu tolto via dai Preti, con dire che quella figura non aveva decoro, né aspetto di santo, stando à sedere con le gambe incavalcate, e co' piedi rozzamente esposti al popolo. Si disperava il Caravaggio per tale affronto nella prima opera da esso pubblicata in chiesa, quando il Marchese Vincenzo Giustiniani si mosse à favorirlo, e liberollo da questa pena; poiché interpostosi con quei Sacerdoti, si prese per sé il quadro, e glie ne fece fare un altro diverso, che è quello che si vede ora sul'altare.[12]*»

All this negativity thrown at poor Caravaggio will remain a key to reading his biography and his works until 2000, up to the denial following the aforementioned study carried out by the Italian Art historian Luigi Spezzaferro.

According to this study, the first version of the work would have been deliberately provisional; in this way Caravaggio

---

[12] "Here happened something, which made a great disturbance, and almost caused Caravaggio to despair with regard to his reputation; since having finished the painting in the middle of St. Matthew and having put it up the altar, was removed by the Priests, saying that that figure had no decoration, nor aspect of a saint, being seated with his legs crossed, and with his feet roughly exposed to the people. Caravaggio was desperate for this affront in the first work published by him in the church, when the Marquis Vincenzo Giustiniani moved to favour him, and free him from this punishment; since interposing with those Priests, he took the picture for himself, and made him make another different one, which is what is now seen on the altar"

would have had plenty of time to create a high-level work and the clients could have used the chapel without giving the impression that it was under construction.

Poor Baglione has not only been heavily teased by Caravaggio and his fellows but is also put in a bad light by Luigi Spezzaferro's research, which has shed light on his badly managed revenge.

Unfortunately, however, Baglione was not the only one to do his utmost in denigrating the Art of the Milanese master. In fact, fourteen years after his death (which took place in 1614) the well-known French painter Nicolas Poussin visited Rome and apostrophized our Caravaggio in an extremely lapidary way:

he had come to destroy Painting.

Poussin may have also been negative in his judgment, but I think something true has said it all in all. After the arrival of Caravaggio, Art has never been the same again; he destroyed the conception of Art to create a form that still echoes in our aesthetic sense and that has thrown the germs for a renewal of painting and theatre.

Another criticism, inexorably dismantled by History, is the one that was addressed to Caravaggio by the Accademia di San Luca founded in 1593 by Federico Zuccari, who held the position of Prince for life of the Academy he founded (the only other artist to have this honour was Antonio Canova).

As *éminence grise* of Italian painting, the mannerist Zuccari was invited to the presentation to the general public of the Contarelli Chapel.

His judgment was not at all commendable:

What noise is this? I see nothing but Giorgione's thought.

The attempt to bring the Caravaggio phenomenon back into the artistic trend that was most popular at the time is a little embarrassing, to be honest. It is difficult not to refute this judgment that would make us believe that Caravaggio is nothing more than a second-order painter, who paints in the manner of other great masters.

One of the major criticisms that were directed to Michelangelo Merisi is due to his uncomprehended style. In an age when the space on a canvas - and also the architectural one - had to be completely filled and saturated with the presence of decorations and characters, it was normal that almost a third of empty and apparently plain canvas could not be accepted.

That extensive presence of the dark background was perceived at the time by the public, which never manages to be open to changes in artistic language, as a real mockery.

Anyone who leaves the established schemes that can guarantee the satisfaction of the public and of the academic rules in force, must undertake an impervious path for acceptance. To put it simply, if you want to be successful you have to give the public what they want, only in this way can you sell; the price of such a quick and rewarding success is expensive: disappear from the History of Art when tastes and fashion change.

The artistic path that Caravaggio has undertaken will bear fruit only in the 20th century! Poor Michelangelo had to be patient with it and in the meantime, he cannot even enjoy the evaluation of his works.

It seems incredible, but for a long time Caravaggio has not talked about it and has been confined to secondary artists. After this long period of oblivion, he was rediscovered, understood and elevated to the honours of Painting. An undoubtedly long path, which today, in our eyes and sensibility, seems to be downright paradoxical.

What turns out to be most curious, however, is not this oblivion on the part of the public but it was the impropriety of the critics, both the contemporary one and the subsequent one.

History sometimes presents us with really curious and not very nice events.

We all know that there were many artists who followed Michelangelo's Art and let themselves be deeply inspired, to the point to be defined as "Caravaggisti"; all this even if Merisi never opened a school or a real workshop and therefore never had real disciples or direct followers.

What is puzzling is to think that while some "pupils" enjoyed a reduced notoriety, thanks to the new way of painting, the master was almost completely forgotten.

In light of all this, I think it is normal to ask how such a thing could have happened.

Justice has its time (and we Italians know it so well) but sooner or later it comes to everyone; a somewhat lean consolation in some situations but that's what we have. Today, finally, we can say that as regards Michelangelo Merisi, known as Caravaggio, justice is done; with all due respect to Baglione and Zuccari who cannot enjoy as much fame today, to be polite and not to say that almost no one remembers them anymore.

Scene IX:
Dead man Walking!

Caravaggio does not have the mentality of a simple artist, engaged in an aesthetic research that can concretize eternal thoughts and sensations; he is also a condemned to death, who lives in his daily life with this situation of total instability, and this has an important influence on his Art.

Lovers of American horror literature have no problem relating Michelangelo's condition to that of John Coffey, the black giant in Stephen King's novel *"The Green Mile"*.

The protagonist of the novel will be executed following the death sentence that was imposed on him, during a distorted trial, for the purely human need to always find a guilty person and a scapegoat in situations of greatest pain and misunderstanding.

The same happens to Caravaggio, even if he - said among us - really has a minimum of guilt.

Stephen King manages to harshly and roughly recreate the unsustainable situation of the condemned man who approaches the room where the sentence will be executed; in the penitentiary of the novel (but also in the real ones), when a prisoner walks for the last time the corridor that will take him to the room, in this case, of the electric chair, there is the echo of these words:

Dead man Walking.

The same phrase was to echo also in the head of poor Michelangelo Merisi. Indeed, in his case the situation to endure was undoubtedly worse: he did not have to flee the executioner but from anyone who met him on the street, since whoever met him was authorized to proceed with the beheading, without incurring any legal problem.

Here the Lombard master's Art becomes a continuous reflection on death and his condition; coming to flow even in requests for grace, invoking mercy several times and on all possible occasions.

His religious-themed Art is a re-enactment of the biblical verses and a manifestation of the teachings of the catechism of the Catholic Church but acquires an intense autobiographical meaning, linked precisely to death.

If we temporarily move to the Borghese Gallery in Rome and stop in front of the *David with the head of Goliath* painted in Naples between 1609 and 1610, we can perfectly realize this strong autobiographical inclination of his works.

Already in the Seventeenth Century the biographers of the Lombard master recognized in the face of the giant Goliath that of Caravaggio himself; fact also confirmed by the most recent criticism as reported by the Art historian Sergio Rossi. Not only that, the painter sending this picture to Cardinal Scipione Borghese, powerful nephew of Pope Paul V, inserts a detail that could not escape the careful sight of the prelate. He is very careful that the letters are read on the blade held by David

H-AS OS

the abbreviation that summarizes the motto of the Order of the Augustinians

Humilitas Occidit Superbiam[13].

---

[13] Humility kills haughtiness

With these words, Caravaggio performs his extreme act of contrition, in the hope that the cardinal will intercede for him with the uncle-pope.

Our Michelangelo has created multiple versions of this work and all of them are characterized by a strong pathos that almost disturbs the observer, who cannot sustain for a long time an intensity of similar emotions. The version in Rome, as we have seen, is the only one to be embellished by the self-portrait of the painter who sees himself as Goliath, while in the version kept at the Kunsthistorsches Museum in Vienna, the model for David is the so much-loved Francesco Boneri (Checco, the servant-lover who lived with him, immortalized in the painter *Amor vincit omnia*).

The presence of the young Boneri perhaps has no particular meaning, it is probably the normal consequence of cohabiting, of always having the boy available for a pose, but in retrospect this assiduous presence of Checco weaves around the artistic production of Caravaggio a dense plot of intimacy autobiography.

In the Roman version there is a more intense and disturbing aspect: Caravaggio sees himself beheaded and dead; portrayed in the part of Goliath. The presence of the painter's head is to be read once again like that of a condemned man asking for forgiveness and who already has clear in mind what his destiny will be if the much-desired grace does not arrive.

Always staying in Rome, let us move to the National Gallery of Ancient Art (the one located in Palazzo Barberini), here is a version of *Judith beading Holofernes*. It is useless to underline the strongly bloody aspect of the scene; we all know the story of Holofernes' beheading and it is easy for us to guess the amount of blood shed in an action like the one represented.

However, this version also wants to tell us another story.

It is enough to be able to read between the lines of the story or, better to say, in this case, between the brush strokes of Caravaggio. Let's look carefully at the work. There are three characters on stage, all mysterious and decidedly fascinating.

Let us focus our attention on the main male character: Holofernes. His body is tense in the spasm of violent death that is inflicted on him. Caravaggio tells us about all his physical pain and above all the psychological horror experienced by man. Nothing overly strange or out of place, as one would expect from the irreverent Milanese painter.

We come now to the two female protagonists of this story. Let us give priority to the more mature character, by etiquette: the old beldam.

All the characteristics of external ugliness, which is to be considered a reflection of internal malice, belong to the woman who holds the towel in anticipation of Holofernes' head. Gimmick that we find in most of the classic tales and fairy tales: the evil and perfidious character is rarely beautiful and if he is, he has operated a magic tweak to improve his appearance.

The younger Judith, on the other hand, has an expression so cold and detached that it gives the impression of being there by chance. Observing with greater attention, there is also the doubt that the young woman is completing a boring task, to which she dedicates herself with disinterest and that she can hardly wait to finish as soon as possible.

Before continuing, the time has come to dispel a myth.

When we find ourselves in front of a work and we are struck by what might seem weak points or, even worse, of more or less gross errors, we must never question its authenticity as a work of Art. A painting that is not exactly as we expect it or that respects the classic canons of tradition and common sense is no less artistic than others perfectly "framed" academically speaking.

In this specific case, despite these details that strike, without a shadow of a doubt, we are facing a true work of Art. What can we understand it from? When can a work be called Art?

A very good question that afflicts the majority of those who deal with Art and who are passionate about it. Yet the answer is easier than you might think: any work, which has at least two different interpretations and both are valid, is a work of Art.

After this small and due digression, let us return to our great work of Art.

Let us look very carefully at Holofernes' face: it is clearly that of Caravaggio; once again the psychological malaise and fear of the condemned to death by beheading returns.

On the other hand, we know very well that Art is a very useful tool to overcome the psychological ailments of artists and also of the public.

We now come to Judith. In this work he has a name and surname: Fillide Melandroni. Her story is also well known to the general public, but it deserves further investigation.

Caravaggio obviously attended the homes of his patrons, the safest way to ingratiate himself with the market, the most important of these distinguished personalities was the banker

Vincenzo Giustiniani. It is precisely at this residence that the Milanese master met his ruin, under the guise of a very charming woman: Fillide. A prostitute who often visited the residences of cardinals and important Roman personalities.

Caravaggio was pleasantly impressed by the beauty of the woman and portrayed her in several works. The two went out together and met in the taverns where the artist used to spend his nights. It is very likely that Caravaggio ended up falling in love with the woman and perhaps began to feel more demanding feelings, perhaps not true love but something very similar and equally intense.

As in any self-respecting love story, this love (or strong infatuation, perhaps) is hindered; Fillide had a "friend" who took very good care of her, since he was also her ponce. He did not welcome the attendance of his Fillide with Caravaggio and tried in all possible and imaginable ways to hinder a possible relationship between the two. At this point in the story, it should be remembered that this man was Ranuccio Tommasoni. Just that Ranuccio Tommasoni.

We all know what happened on 28th May 1606: Caravaggio responded to Ranuccio's provocations and killed him.

That crime triggered the series of events that will drag Caravaggio into the whirlpool that has gradually destroyed and annihilated him.

Now, read from a biographical point of view, the work acquires a decidedly deeper and more dramatic meaning. The fact that it is precisely the woman who was the trigger of the painter's death sentence that cut the head of Holofernes-Caravaggio is particularly significant.

If we look at the canvas, now, with greater attention and sensitivity, we cannot fail to make our own the most plausible key to interpretation: this scene look like a nightmare from which Caravaggio-Holofernes would like to wake up.

The position of Holofernes-Caravaggio, his arms stretched in an effort to lift the torso from the mattress, his mouth open in a scream; it seems that the protagonist is waking up from the nightmare in which he saw the woman who was the cause of his ruin intent on cutting off his head.

Not so much a biblical scene, as a real painted nightmare, in order to exorcise his greatest fear and to soften the public official in the hope of obtaining the long-awaited grace.

That's why the woman gives the impression of being extraneous to the scene and does not seem emotionally involved at all. To tell the truth, it is very difficult to believe that a woman, who is cutting the head of a man, seems so uninterested in the action and does not even make a great physical effort. Judith-Fillide is more of a presence, one of the three characters from a nightmare.

A big bad dream that we know will never become reality but that will make the painter's life a continuous escape to get away from that horror until the day of his death, which occurred in a somewhat suspicious way.

Let us continue our journey now and move to the island of Malta and to be precise in the capital Valletta, where the Saint John's Co-Cathedral is located.

Here we find one of the most intense works of Caravaggio, especially if read from a biographical point of view: *The Beheading of St. John the Baptist*.

The religious theme of this painting is well known and easy to interpret; obviously (we must never forget it) it is easily interpretable by all those who have received a minimum Christian teaching. After Salome's request, following her bewitching dance of the seven veils for the lustful stepfather, the Baptist's head must be delivered to her on a silver tray, not so much to make the sadistic dancer happy but to make the vindictive mother happy.

Caravaggio decided to represent the saint in the final and most intense moment of the beheading. The scene has a very strong emotional impact and although it seems to respect all the canons of painting (of the time) it has many curious and unusual aspects.

Personally, for our Caravaggio this work has an invaluable value, it will be thanks to this painting with such important dimensions (3.61 x 5.20 m!) that he will receive the Maltese Cross. A parenthesis of happiness that is destined to last a short time, unfortunately.

One wonders what he did this time. Let us go in order.

History tells us that following the recognition of such an important honour by the order, Caravaggio flees suddenly and quickly from the island. For a "coincidence" that leaves amazed, after his escape, the knights read the papal bull that decreed its cancellation from the order, a reading that took place right in front of the picture.

Much has been said about the composition of the work, which remains truly unique and not only for its size (it is the largest painting created by the Lombard artist) but also and above all for some decidedly risky compositional choices.

Let us refresh our memories of the historical tale of the painting. Saint John the Baptist is in prison because he has publicly attacked power and is awaiting his sentence. The woman to whom he addressed, in front of everyone, as a "bad 'un" is very vindictive and uses the attractiveness of her daughter (to whom the "husband" is not indifferent) to obtain the preacher's head.

Now let us look at the picture, starting right from the setting. We are on the street, of the prison we probably only see the door and a window where we can see two jailers or curious prisoners. A knight observes the operation indicating the basin for the head and two servants (probably employed in the palace) are desperate while the executioner has already dealt the blow and is preparing to finish the work for which he is paid.

Apparently, everything is normal and the representation could be obvious and easily accessible for everyone, despite a slight anachronism and a detail in the setting that go almost unnoticed: the clothes that do not date back to the time of the event and the place, where we find a building that from the facade is reminiscent of central Renaissance Italy.

Yet, if we carefully and silently observe the work, we begin to perceive the feeling that the centre of the representation is neither the saint who took off nor one of the co-protagonist actors. The fulcrum of the composition, structured in such a way that our eyes fall right there at that precise point, is the misericorde.

For those unfamiliar with beheadings, it is fair to remember that the knife that the executioner holds in his hand behind his back is called misericorde, in fact.

Obviously, it is a detail that has not escaped the careful observation of many experts and critics, the fact that in Italian the name of this weapon is *Misericordia* and it also means mercy. According to a widely held opinion, the presence of this special knife is to be interpreted as a further plea to obtain the much-hoped grace (which can only be obtained through an act of mercy, in fact) according to his death sentence. The knife was used by executioners to hurriedly deliver the coup de grace to the death row inmate whose execution may not have had an immediate outcome; many professionals of capital executions (perhaps due to lack of experience or simply because it was not a good day) were unable to kill the condemned at the first shot and so the culprit suffered beyond due, to put an end to this unjust condition and extreme pain he intervened with the mercy by cutting the nerve endings still connected, thus resulting in a faster death.

This weapon could have different shapes and could also be used in other contexts but the function, essentially, remained the same. Some misericorde were made in the shape of a stiletto and were used in war; after a battle they passed between the dead and the wounded left on the field and put an end to the suffering of those who had suffered injuries so serious that they could no longer be cured in any way, sticking the stiletto in their hearts.

Now that we know all about misericorde, let's go back to our picture.

Several Art historians see in this painted object a plea for grace by Caravaggio, who is in a precarious situation due to the sentence relating to the killing of Ranuccio Tommasoni; remember that the execution could be performed by anyone who met him even on the street and this made the Milanese master experience a situation of absolute uncertainty and terror (not surprisingly, the scene portrayed is on the street and not in the prisons where it should have been made).

Other historians, however, want to see in the weapon at the centre of the representation an easier reference (by simple assonance) to the name of the company that commissioned the work: the Confraternity of Mercy, in fact.

The latter is a possible and perhaps probable explanation; however, it remains a little too superficial and banal if we link it to Caravaggio's way of operating, which was not too easily satisfied with commonplaces.

In my opinion, there is a detail in the picture that goes in favour of the vision linked to his death sentence. If we look carefully we can see that the blood, which spurts from the wound inflicted with the sword to cut the saint's head, creates a small puddle on the floor; under which you can see the painter's signature which is written with the blood of the innocent, unjustly sentenced to death.

Since Caravaggio had been named Knight of Graces shortly before receiving the commission for this work, he will sign:

F Michelangelo

where the F stands for "Frà" (in Italian it means brother). It is this particular, in addition to its extraordinary dimensions, that makes the work a unique work in Merisi's artistic biography.

The detail is not negligible.

The blood of an innocent person, sentenced to capital punishment by beheading, takes the form of the letters that make up the name of another person sentenced to the same sentence.

One wonders: Michelangelo Merisi, known as Caravaggio, denies the evidence of guilt and still declares himself innocent or was he really innocent, the victim of an injustice?

We cannot have certain answers, of course, but only our personal interpretations in retrospect, which we can expose but still remain our visions, strictly personal.

There is no doubt that Caravaggio was guilty of the killing of Tommasoni, that he considered himself a victim of the situation (created by others) and not of his violent nature is equally clear. That he had convinced himself that he was an innocent martyr and wanted to convince others too is evident in his works.

Scene X:
Like Oscar

Beauty is such an abstract and indefinite concept that it is difficult to find a common definition in different cultures; it is possible to affirm that there is no possibility of understanding in the cultures that colour the world. The definitions that are given at times, even, are in contrast with each other. Yet it is not a presence extraneous to our life, so much so that we can be easily surrounded and often even overwhelmed.

Legend has it that colossal film wars were fought because of Beauty; Beauty lovers went bankrupt, others were killed or ended up in prison. From Helen of Troy to the hypothesized theft of a Riace bronze, everyone (both the good and the bad) have endangered or embarrassed themselves in order to possess Beauty.

If on the one hand we realize that a universal definition of Beauty is almost impossible in itself, it is not out of place to associate it with pleasure, which obviously can have a more physical or more mental connotation based on its field of action.

In the imagination of all of us, the person who has become the emblem of the one who has been overwhelmed by Beauty and who has declared that the only way to resist a temptation is to surrender to it is Oscar Wilde. The great English poet because of his unconditional love for Beauty and for the pleasure that derives from it ended up in prison.

Caravaggio did not have a very different fate, as we well know.

His paintings never miss an opportunity to tell us about his passion for female and male beauty, his life tells us the beauty of the luxuries of aristocratic palaces all around Italy and his love for the transgression that led him to live a nightlife, like a real rock star, between excesses and loss of control.

It is difficult to find an artist (in the true sense of the term, not a simple someone who deals in some way with the creation of objects inappropriately considered artistic) who has not suffered due to the path taken towards Beauty.

Why put in jail an aesthete or judge it improper to have sought beauty in situations considered unorthodox by common thought?

The answer is not that difficult, all things considered.

The search for Beauty has more to do with ethics than with morality, that's why it is easily attackable and judged by anyone.

This is a somewhat difficult topic, I realize; let us make it clearer, by being helped by the Art of Caravaggio himself. First, allow me a notional parenthesis.

Morality is a highly variable aspect in the life of a human being; it is imposed by society and religion and contemplates a whole series of rules to follow in order to live and be accepted in a specific group. If we think of the etymology of this word (from the Latin *moràlia*) we have precisely the indication of existence led by a series of rules that indicate how man should behave. Obviously, based on the historical period, the prevailing culture and the dominant religion, morality can change and within the context of the same civilization it can undergo strong changes over the centuries or millennia.

Ethics, on the other hand, remains a more personal aspect, it is not imposed from the outside and therefore it is truer for the individual. It has to do with the research that each individual put in place in order to find one or more criteria that allow him to manage his freedom and has as its object all those moral values that determine the values of the individual himself. Ethics allows us to find the meaning of existing as individuals, its most intrinsic meaning and to better define the meaning of one's own and the universe that surrounds it.

Seen from this point of view, the Art of Caravaggio becomes pure and simple expression of his intimate and sincere ethics.

The world of Merisi is easily readable in his paintings. The search for the physical Beauty that goes through his Painting between fatal and handsome women and graceful and young boys. The sense of forbidden and transgressive that transpires from the shadows illuminated by the light of candles, a constant rebellion against the conventions of that well-off and well-thought society in which he lived, which underneath in his own intimacy (in the darkness of their true being) has always hatched great transgression.

All this can only resonate as an echo for all of us who have been lucky enough to know the great English aesthete, Oscar Wilde.

What unites these two great artists separated by almost three centuries of history is not only their spasmodic search for pleasure through beauty but also the narration. Both, in fact, have found sustenance thanks to their artistic skills (Caravaggio painting and Wilde writing) and the public has appreciated their stories but, we must admit, also their biographies. Thus, Oscar was also invited overseas to tell his life and his ideas (which we can also consider a real-life philosophy) and Caravaggio aroused the public's attention not only for the skill with which he made his works or for his rupture style but also, and above all, for his personal vision of the world and of the reality that animates each of his brushstrokes and scenes represented.

The common aspects between the two artists did not end here, there would still be one, to be honest.

Both created an aura of interest around their person and entered fully into the common imagination of the public by exerting an ever-stronger ascendant.

There is no doubt that someone can also find them attractive; this is not simply due to their physical appearance but is a consequence of the cursed character who sewed on themselves and who survives thanks to the chronicles and their works, real immortal classics even if sometimes they are seasoned by a hint of immorality.

ACT TWO

Scene I:
The light that creates

One cannot speak of Caravaggio's Art without taking into consideration the real great protagonist of his pictorial research: light.

Many have gone out of their way to describe the uniqueness of his technique in making this perennial tension between shadow and light; some made a gross mistake defining it static.

It is anything but static.

The bodies and faces of the protagonists, as well as the environments - even if enveloped by shadow - take shape and consistency thanks to the continuous modelling of light, which seems to take the black and formless material of which Merisi's canvases are made and create all that which is necessary by modelling and shaping it to your liking.

Although the background of Caravaggio is mainly dark, tending to black, it is not so easy to copy it. To tell the truth, the best that anyone who tries to copy his works can get is getting closer to the original. The complexity of Caravaggio's background lies in the fact that it is not plain.

The effect that is created on the canvases is that of multiple glazes, real shades of different browns, which overlapping create what only the Lombard painter has managed to give us. As we will see in the following chapters, Caravaggio's influence goes far beyond his contemporaries and can also be seen in contemporary Art; an example above all is the work of Ettore Spalletti, who creates works striving to create a colour that is as natural (and tending to true) as possible and therefore not monotonous (intended mono-tone), like his famous blue. This aspect is easily observable in nature, if we think of the colour of the sky, we will never find it perfectly solid but it will have areas of greater intensity of colour and others of greater clarity. The same goes for the darkness we can go through at night.

The "black" background of Caravaggio would be defined more correctly using the plural: the "black" backgrounds of Caravaggio.

The correct reading of its bituminous black background, which is the background to most of his works, is what leads us to consider it a set of soft lights and deep shadows.

Caravaggio developed his personal study of light and pictorial technique thanks also to the camera obscura, which allowed him to obtain unique results for his time and remain amazing even today.

This tool is, in all respects, the direct ancestor of the camera.

A real wooden magic box in which the world enters through a hole, is reflected inside and offered to the viewer through a second hole to which the eye must approach.

Caravaggio is not a simple painter, he is also a photographer and he portrays on his canvases the images reflected by the camera obscura. Although it seems like a play upon words, his works are images of the reflected images of reality. Thanks to the use of this tool, Caravaggio's faces and still lives enjoy a very special light and particularly delicate outlines. The use of the camera obscura and the use of colour according to the lessons of the Venetian School make his painting a unique event that few have managed to imitate even remotely.

Caravaggio's attention and virtuosity towards light have reached extreme levels. In order to paint with the right light, which would fall from above, illuminating the scene - with an extremely theatrical optical effect - our painter even went so far as to make a hole in the ceiling of the studio where he worked. Easy to imagine the joy of the landlord.

An extremely interesting aspect of Caravaggio's painting is the presence of light but not in general and normal terms, here we must in all respects consider it theatrical. As said before, Merisi was not a simple painter, he was an *ante litteram* photographer as well as being an excellent theatrical director.

Compared to the modern Art of the Sixteenth and Seventeenth Centuries, the Art of the late Nineteenth and early

Twentieth Century was enriched by the esoteric and psychoanalytic culture; despite this turn, much of Caravaggio's vision has survived, reaching the present day. Above all the world lit up by the light of candles.

His candlelight has left a mark so strong in painting that it lasted a long time in the common imagination of other painters who made it such a distinctive feature of their Art that it became part of their name: Gerrit van Honthrost is remembered with the Italianized name of Gherardo delle Notti ("Gerard of the nights").

If we run in memory to Chalon's masterpiece dedicated to the sorceress Circe, we find a very Caravaggio-way echo as regards the lighting of the scene.

The change is exciting if you think of the first night scene painted in the History of Art by the great master Piero della Francesca who in his dream of Constantine creates a very bright, almost diurnal night. Obviously managing to give an idea of the nocturnal even if very bland, but having been the precursor of this style we can well excuse it for some inaccuracy committed (just as we have to justify the coarse errors of Buonarroti in the Sistine Chapel). With Caravaggio the night is overcome, it is not only that black expanse, heavy as only the dark can be, but it is also dark light; which here becomes a kind of black matter, formless and which can be shaped by light becoming everything. With Michelangelo Merisi, in fact, black presents itself as the result of the whole, all the colours merge on its palette, losing any value of "colour" because Caravaggio makes it a real matter.

If the light of Caravaggio were a marble, static and eternal presence (as some historians and critics mistakenly consider it) Merisi's works would have a minimal visual impact.

And as we all know, this is not the case. Indeed, it is exactly the opposite.

Caravaggio's light creates. It moves sinuously between the folds of the dark background and makes the figures come out of the bituminous mass. If it were static, it would not create but would highlight simple lines and colours.

Today, on theatre stages, the light follows the same concept. Oblique as in *The Calling of St. Matthew*, it gives the right depth to the scene. The light is intelligent - both in Caravaggio's works and in the theatre - falling exactly where it must fall and illuminating the characters and props. It always has the right intensity and is never violent, we are still far from those nervous and cutting effects of colour that will prevail in the Art of the Twentieth century but the emotional intensity is perhaps stronger.

Scene II:
Masterful black

After having talked about Caravaggio's famous light, we cannot fail to consider the second main actor of his works: black.

One of the most representative characteristics of Michelangelo Merisi are his backgrounds, which contrast with the intensity of the light.

We should understand what were the reasons that led him to change the shades used, in fact at the beginning of his career we do not find such a bituminous palette.

If we take into consideration its famous *Basket of Fruit* (which has been chosen in the past to decorate the banknote of the ancient Italian 100,000 liras), we find that type of background that does not allow us to have precise indications on time (at what time of day are we?) and place (where we are?). It almost seems that Caravaggio anticipated De Chirico's metaphysical painting with a few centuries in advance!

Although it may seem impossible, the picture, unfortunately, had not been much liked by the public of the time. For how many romantic stories we want to tell, the work has travelled a lot, rolled up in the painter's bag, before finding a collector who bought it (and consequently launched the career of the Lombard master).

The irony of fate wants this work - characterized mainly by light and bright tones - to end up in the collection of the family of that saint who will turn off the light in the Art of the Milanese school.

As we know, St. Charles Borromeo was a unique character in the religious and cultural landscape in Northern Italy. His commitment to thwart the Reformation is worthy of the most tenacious leader. With strokes of Calvaries, anathemas and books did his utmost to ensure that the Reformed were less attractive in the eyes of the faithful; thus, avoiding a mass conversion in favour of those who protested on the other side of the Alps.

The personality of St. Charles Borromeo is decidedly complicated but even more intriguing. His relationships with women were not very relaxed and easy, on the one hand he almost seemed to have a deep hatred for the fairer sex and on the other it is known that he had helped poor girls to get a dowry in order to find a husband and was extremely protective in towards his sisters.

Another very difficult relationship with contrasting characters was the one with culture.

The drive that made the agricultural and provincial Milan become an internationally recognized centre for Italian industry and fashion is also partly due to the Counter-Reformation and the cultural strategies implemented by St. Charles Borromeo. It is no coincidence that one of the symbols attributed to him is a book; the well-known San Carlone of Arona (a colossus dedicated to St. Charles) represents in its over 30 meters high the saint holding a large book in his hand.

St. Charles, together with his cousin Federico, undertook a series of changes that facilitated the development of culture in the Lombard capital: from the opening to the public of the Ambrosiana Library, to that of numerous seminaries up to the decorations on the floor of the Cathedral. This commitment was aimed above all at the diffusion of culture in a more or less transversal way in society. Everyone had to be able to understand and access knowledge. But not in a personal and free way as was the case for Protestants; knowledge had to be always and only filtered by appropriate and specially prepared organs - according to San Carlo - and that could act as a guide: the Church, in the people of the specially educated clergy, obviously.

This cultural revolution presented a high price in the end (even during construction, to be honest). Although the real commitment to the diffusion of culture has allowed greater access to knowledge, we cannot forget that free thought has been heavily suffocated and conditioned.

In his rigid and dedicated mind, St. Charles saw in the excessive presence of colours, in too many festive possibilities and in the new ideas that a dangerous enemy was spreading in Europe.

So, Lombard Painting has gradually become darker and has played more and more on the warm earth tones combined more and more with black: an elegant, chaste colour that lessens the senses.

St. Charles' thoughts on social life and Art can easily be summarized in this way: by removing any possible incentive there is no risk of committing sin.

All the beautiful colours of Michelangelo Buonarroti, of Perugino, all the Sienese school of the Thirteenth Century and the Beauty of the colours of the Venetian school were suffocated; oppressed by an increasingly present and oppressive black.

Read yes, but under the guidance of an expert who can lead you towards the right understanding of the text. This was Borromeo's answer to the innovations required by the Reformation.

Culture often goes hand in hand with freedom; from the time of the Greeks to the present day, they are inviting us more and more knowledge to be truly free. Dear old Seneca has been telling us since the First Century:

Be a servant of knowledge if you want to be truly free.

During the Counter-Reformation period this basic aspect of human freedom was not changed, only one new actor was added to the process: the knowledge had to be that presented and organized by the competent authorities.

It is in this cultural and religious-political environment that Caravaggio's palette acquires those shades that have made it famous all over the world and that continues to fascinate us.

At the beginning of his pictorial career, Michelangelo Merisi holds in his hands a palette with shades strongly oriented towards light and bright colours and winked at the great masters who had preceded him, as it was right that it was obviously. Nobody can afford the luxury of taking their first steps in Art without relying on those who have preceded it and with whom one has a certain affinity.

Over time, his style has become increasingly defined. This is obviously a more than natural process in the evolution of an artist and the use of colours has also changed with style. Usually, style changes are influenced by the artist's new way of seeing the world and wanting to represent it; as we have seen, however, in this specific case it was an imposition of change dictated by external factors.

As we have previously seen, Caravaggio was not that "tavern bird" that is often believed to have been. His life was also nocturnal but some of his friends lived in luxurious palaces and competed with the sword and political games for the power in the mosaic of duchies, republics and kingdoms that was Italy before unification.

And Caravaggio knew how to move skilfully in these environments. The prevailing ideas in terms of culture also became his ideas, the needs expressed by the power to teach the masses found in him a worthy divulger. His constant winking at strong powers will lead him to respect their diktats, while criticizing them, sometimes even very harshly.

And so, his palette loses its colours.

The dense and suffocating bituminous black takes over in his canvases and meets the approval of the promoters of the new political-religious ideas. But he can't help putting something of his own ideas.

If on the one hand black dominates, on the other we have a substantial increase in the intensity of the surviving colours. The cause of these bright colours does not seem to be a conscious choice of the painter but a necessary compensation required by the light itself.

As always, Caravaggio knows how to be irreverent and brilliant!

Black is no longer a punishment; in the paintings by Caravaggio it is so heavy, like a formless material that is shaped by the action of light, but it is a presence that gradually becomes more and more hypnotic and bewitches us. If we take the sweet *Sleeping Cupid* of Palazzo Pitti we can realize this aspect.

The body of the little Cupid seems to come out of the black mass of the background, it is shaped by the light and we have the sensation of feeling its whole body.

An intense and creative light.

A good starting point to be able to think freely, beyond any convention.

Scene III:
The beggars

A habitual and important presence in Caravaggio's painting is that of the poor, figures who are often present in the History of Art and who have their own particular biography.

It is not difficult to imagine the anger of smart society as they observe in the works of Caravaggio certain soles of dirty feet in the foreground or poorly mended and worn clothes, not to mention the hands and faces covered with dirt and careless.

Who knows then the comments when the public realized they knew perfectly well the name and profession of the deceased model who impersonated the Virgin Mary in the picture that immortalizes his passing away (we will talk about this in the next chapter).

The presence of the most disadvantaged part of society is not only and exclusively due to the personal sensitivity of our painter or his desire to transgress but is part of a real historical moment.

The Sixteenth and Seventeenth Centuries are characterized by a daily life also and above all made of poverty. These two centuries have seen long wars, epidemics and famines; these were not easy years and many people fell into the blackest misfortune.

This scourge has affected all Europe and we can only imagine how it has affected the mentality of society in a transversal way. Based on data provided by some historians we can easily understand that the situation was not only difficult but bordered on a large scale. In fact, it has been estimated that around 20% of a city's population was made up of beggars. Such an exponential increase in the poor was also due to the fact that many landowners had started to expel the peasants depriving them of the lands they worked and consequently the only chance they had of being able to maintain and feed their families.

From northern Europe came very rigid and harsh ideas, which put people who had to survive in some way despite economic hardships in even more complicated situations. First the poor were deprived of their few properties and then, in the Seventeenth Century, they were even put in prison. All this could only lead to an outbreak of violence, epidemics, thefts, robberies and scams.

We are facing not only an economic crisis but also of social security. All of Northern European painting is sensitive to this phenomenon. The greatest masters of the time painted scenes in which vagabonds and poor beggars make their appearance, always when they were not themselves the main protagonists of the scenes.

It is in this social atmosphere that Painting also moves, among the most important and well-known names in the artistic panorama of this era we can remember the great Rembrandt while among the less known to the general public Adriaen van Ostade, Pieter van der Heyden and Jan Steen.

And it is in this environment that Caravaggio finds impetus for his Art.

If we take his famous *Pilgrim's Madonna* (or Madonna of Loreto) - painted between 1603 and 1605 and kept in the Basilica of Sant'Agostino in Campo Marzio in Rome - we can better understand this aspect.

The pilgrim couple represented on their knees before the Virgin is clearly made up of extremely poor people. Moreover, the picture is very interesting; the Virgin seems to have appeared on the street to see who rang the doorbell, as if the two pilgrims had passed by to greet or leave some publication to read.

The scene seems to be taken from a film or a theatrical representation and as we have already seen, in Caravaggio, nothing is left to chance. The Lombard master's need for realism reaches levels that do not even allow him to adapt, albeit minimally, to the pictorial tradition that has always appreciated the virtuous effort to mask the physiognomy of the models that lent themselves to pose for the realization of the works; in this way it is possible to have the feeling that the protagonists of the works were people in flesh and blood, with real appearances, even if they belonged to myth or religion. The model disappeared and turned into the real Bacchus and the model lost her true personality to become the Virgin Mary.

Knowing Caravaggio, the massive presence of so many poor people in his works is not a simple coincidence or an artist whim. To better understand his tendency, we have to pay attention to his biography, especially to the environments in which he lived during the day and to those where he took refuge at night. If, moreover, we keep in mind his character so unaccustomed to conformism, we can well understand the reasons for his choices.

In a respectable and socially elevated environment, which has decided to take Baroque as the dominant style in architecture to hide and fill moral and ethical shortcomings, the almost irreverent presence of the less wealthy society is to be understood as a criticism of society itself, a criticism with an almost jester-like flavour.

Since the Middle Ages, the jester was the only person authorized in the whole court to be able to criticize and deride - always with due modalities - the power, represented by the maximum local offices, up to the king. His criticisms were never taken too seriously, even if they were based on proven truths, and led the audience to laugh at themselves, reflecting.

We assume that Caravaggio's genius is decidedly cumbersome. His attitude is that of a rock star, at night we find him intent on living in the most intense and over the top way while in the daytime every opportunity is good to break something or someone.

This attitude of his is also faithfully reflected in his art; so, we see Virgins who look like housewives on the doorstep or impersonated (unconsciously) by prostitutes on the table of their own funeral vigil. Not to mention the dirty feet to which we have already referred; let us think of the jolts that these images must have created in the audience of the time, making blasphemy cry and causing dissension.

Before continuing, at this point, a brief note is a must: fairness requires that no one put words in Caravaggio's mouth that perhaps he has never uttered or attribute to him thoughts that are not his; for the record, too many thinkers, historians and critics are so convinced of their ideas that they are directly attributed to the thought of an artist.

Let us go back to Caravaggio.

I personally believe that his stylistic decisions and the use of certain subjects were mainly a way to go against respectability and old-fashioned thought that prevailed (and continues to dictate, still today) among our local public.

From the first brushstroke to the last, Michelangelo Merisi wanted to impose his presence, breaking the classicism prevailing in the mentalities of his contemporaries. That's why we should think, in my opinion, that his prostitutes and his poor are nothing more than the style of the most aesthetic provoker of the entire Art History.

His provocations should be considered as such. Whoever wants to see a social, and even theological, message in his canvases, I believe is definitely off course. Caravaggio will be out of the box until the end and his works must be observed with a vision outside the box and consequently the interpretation to be pursued cannot be delimited by the classical canons. "Outside the box" should be the key to use to get in touch with this excellent master.

The presentation to the public of one of his works must have been something really funny. The public: rich old fogey, full of lace and with hair in order, with movements that conveyed all their social superiority, they observed in ecstasy well-paid canvases. The subjects: the people whom the wealthy on the street avoided like the plague, maybe even bringing a handkerchief to the nose so as not to breathe the smell that disgusted them so much.

By identifying with this situation, perhaps, we can understand all the artistic and rupture charge of the Lombard master.

And even if not completely, we can have fun with him.

Scene IV:
That Virgin that everyone knew

Among the many works by Caravaggio, there is a very nice one; not for the scene told as for the choices of our painter.

Before the usual controversy arises: the work was not stolen but regularly purchased.

The painting was commissioned by the Discalced Carmelites who, after seeing it finished, rejected it, and all in all we should not be very surprised at this fact. What can allow us to begin to understand his artistic value, however, is the fact that the enlightened Duke of Mantua -

always attentive to culture and artistic innovations - bought it on the recommendation of that Rubens that we all know for be an eminent painter and also a good diplomat.

The Gonzaga court, as we all know, was quite expensive and the finances often settled on the negative sign. In order to balance their budgets, the Dukes were forced to alienate their fantastic collection which was acquired by Charles I of England. Upon the death of the sovereign, it was decided to sell a large part of his collection which was bought by Everhard Jabach, a wealthy French banker, who subsequently decided to sell everything to Louis XIV of France; among the paintings in this collection was obviously our *Death of the Virgin*.

After much wandering the picture was hung on the walls of the Louvre where it still rests today.

Let us now return to the renunciation by the Discalced Carmelites, after recovering from the shock following the vision of the painting.

First of all, we must realize that the issue is extremely delicate. In the canonical gospels the death of the Virgin is never mentioned, as far as we know, she would have fallen asleep deeply and would have been taken directly, body and soul, to heaven. So, technically, the Virgin is spared the passing away and the subsequent wait for the Judgment (both personal and universal) as it will be for all of us ordinary mortals.

Caravaggio does not miss the opportunity to create scandal.

In his work he decided to show us the dead Virgin and just to show us all his intention, the title clearly states the word death. Caravaggio, in doing so, borders on the apocryphal gospels, which for many members of the counter-reformed clergy are a bit of a bogeyman.

Merisi chooses to represent a human death, modelled by a dense light of existential anguish and a lugubrious nostalgia.

Longhi, on this picture, writes:

... the anguish of these bystanders takes on infinite sense and authority from the devastating glow that, breaking from the left into the circle of colours already strangely flaming and while fighting with all the species of the shadow, pause for a moment on the upturned face of the dead Madonna, on baldness lunate, on the throbbing necks, on the unmade hands of the apostles; slashes John's sore face sideways; makes the Magdalene seat a single luminous block; of his hand on the knee only a clot of clotted light.

What is even more destabilizing is that the mystical symbols are almost completely absent, giving the impression that we are facing a common scene and not a representation that involves the divinity. Only by carefully observing the characters, can we realize that the Virgin is characterized by a very thin and almost imperceptible halo.

In an era when the public (of any social background) paid close attention to the interpretation of symbols because they were an important channel for transmitting information, these details certainly did not go unnoticed. So much transgression could only create problems for our Caravaggio. Obviously, the canvas was removed, it could not remain in a sacred place to suggest scandalous ideas and was replaced by an equal but more orthodox subject signed by Carlo Saraceni, a Venetian painter who was unable to instil a minimum of scandal even in his more erotic scene between *Mars and Venus* today at Thyssen-Bornemisza Museum in Madrid.

The situation is then aggravated, just for a change, by his character and so the painter is forced in a hurry to pack up and run away from Rome; it was when during one of his usual quarrels for more or less futile reasons he killed Ranuccio Tommasoni.

This picture is a riot of impropriety, if we go back to observe it carefully we can realize that its setting also has something improper.

Traditionally, we are used to seeing the Virgin, alive and well, who is lifted off the ground by some angels and carried upwards. It is definitely the best way to convey the idea of a *dormitio*, a deep sleep, and not of a hypothetical human death. In some cases, the apostles are silent all around an empty or flower-filled tomb (symbol of rebirth).

Caravaggio paints the apostles around the funeral table in deep condolence. The scene is (obviously) dark, the red cloth increases the fatal and painful sensation. The lifeless body of the Virgin is resting on a table which, for the occasion, has been softened by what appears to be a voluminous cushion or folded fabrics.

The image deliberately and clearly recalls the funeral vigils that were celebrated by ordinary people in the taverns. To which, most likely, Caravaggio had attended, not a few times.

The red dress of the Virgin is another nice mystery.

Of all the Marian colours that could be used to identify the character, the Lombard master chose one that is not exactly very traditional.

If with a little effort of imagination, we move to the moment when the work was revealed to the public, it should not be difficult to see the mouths open in amazement and the eyes widened in disbelief. Partly, of course, because of the beauty of the work but above all because many knew the Virgin by name (perhaps surname) and profession. In fact, according to some historians, the woman represented in the features of the Virgin was a well-known Roman prostitute found drowned in the Tiber. Others, however, perhaps driven by the strong respect for a similar subject want to recognize in the Virgin's features those of Lena, the model of Caravaggio, who by profession (however) was a courtesan.

The theory of the corpse found in the river should have greater credibility, since it would be testified and proven by the suspected swelling of the woman's belly.

The interpretation of the work and the symbols "hidden" by the painter in his canvases has always caused an incessant run of ink, sometimes even unnecessarily. Everyone seems to have something to say and so many are the custodians of an illuminating truth, which, however, seems sometimes to be weak.

If we start from the presence of the large red cloth that closes the scene, we hear the echo of the words curtain and theatre. For the umpteenth time we are faced with the Caravaggio's conception of representation in Painting as a theatrical scene.

Assuming that the table is that of an inn, that the woman is a prostitute drowned in the Tiber and that Magdalene has been called as an appearance by the express will of the director, since her presence is not contemplated in the normal Christian iconography, one wonders how to interpret this picture?

Despite his strong rebellious sense, it seems too exaggerated to think of blasphemy; he may have been a bad boy from a good family who enjoyed making disasters here and there but I think it is a bit too much to think that Caravaggio wanted to disrespect the figure of the Virgin. If only for more commercial calculations if not for an innate respect for the divinity.

The solution to the puzzle could be a little simpler.

In these years, as we have seen, the moderation of the costumes is promoted and luxury is no longer viewed favourably. Even legends say that St. Charles Borromeo and his cousin Federico lived in poverty to set a good example; I use the word legends because the correspondence with the family shows St. Charles attentive to the image and the clothes that had to be changed if worn and in not very good condition.

Let us go back to our history, remembering that the key word for the society of the time was simplicity and moderation. Michelangelo Merisi receives the commission for a painting with the *dormitio* of the Virgin as subject.

Realizing the work, he is struck by an idea: paint the scene in a very simple and poor place. It probably takes inspiration from a memory: a funeral wake which he had attended a few days before.

That the deceased was a prostitute does not matter to the director, the actor on stage loses his biography and becomes only and exclusively the character to whom he must breathe life with his stage presence.

Subversive yes, but without exaggerating too much going to blasphemy.

The character of Mary Magdalene?

Even if she was not there ichnographically, the director thought it right that there was, for greater completeness and for the visual (and conceptual) balance on the stage.

Scene V:
A little bit of gossip

Sometimes, even too often, it seems that the Art in which the public best juggles (and some self-styled historians) is that of gossip.

Let us see how this, sometimes questionable practice, can affect the way we observe Art.

Among the experts there are two important lines of thought. There are those who see an artist in the biography of an indispensable element in order to understand his artistic life and those who, on the other hand, demonize the biographical life because it could unnecessarily suffocate the artist's thought and uniqueness.

According to an adage that is lost, now, in the mists of time, the truth lies in the middle.

I firmly believe that knowing the biography of an artist is indispensable for the period that passes from the modern era up to us and that it is irrelevant in the case of many artists from the modern era going back to the Palaeolithic.

When the artist disappears behind the veil of the subject to be represented and the historical, theological and social interpretations that others commission him, we can easily see his works of Art without knowing what he ate or which kind of music he listened to.

Speaking, however, of artists who bring their thinking into play and who manage for good or bad to translate their personal point of view into a work, with or without commission, I think it is very important to know their thought and life; otherwise, important data for understanding artistic choices would be lacking.

The personal judgment of an artist's private life is quite another thing. An artist should never be stigmatized for the choices made in his life, which should not even be reported in the pages of interpretation or artistic criticism.

Michelangelo Merisi was the man and could be judged because of his lifestyle choices; provided that it has some utility and that it is up to us to judge it. Caravaggio is the artist and as such must be considered, completely split from his alter ego Merisi.

Caravaggio cannot be judged for his *Amor vincit omnia*; on Merisi's lifestyle, however, we could discuss and talk about, provided there is nothing better to do.

The painting cited is among the greatest masterpieces of the painter and it is difficult to find someone who does not appreciate it or who is not ecstatic looking at it.

Let us get to know a little better the history of this magnificent work preserved today at the Gemäldegalerie (Gallery of paintings, in German) in Berlin.

The title of the work is an Italianized Latin phrase that can be translated as "Love wins over everything" by the famous Publius Vergilius Maro, better known simply as Virgil. The exact words of the verse of the poet from Mantua are

Omnia vincit amor et nos cedamus amori[14].

Our sentence

Amor vincit omnia

it follows a little the Italian construction that wants to start the sentence with the subject, in this Latin language gives much more freedom, but in itself the meaning does not change.

---

[14] Love wins everything, and we give in to love

As often happens in completing a painter's catalogue, it is not easy to have a precise indication of the year of creation of the painting. Experts must therefore sharpen the view, pick up on the canvas every little nuance and detail that can give an indication in order to date the work. Dating is often decided based on the development of the artist's style or the use of certain colours.

Or, just read some books.

Reading three madrigals written in 1603 by Gaspare Murtola (poet born in Genoa around 1570 and died in Tarquinia in 1624) we can find clear and explicit references to this Caravaggio's work. Other references are made during the trial, also in 1603, brought by poor Giovanni Baglione against Caravaggio and his friends. During the trial it is pointed out that the Baglione had created a painting that represented a

amor devino[15]

and that he was a sort of competitor to a

amor terreno[16]

---

[15] Ancient Italian words for "divine love"

[16] Ancient Italian words for "earthly love"

made by Caravaggio.

The painting by the Lombard master was commissioned by Marquis Vincenzo Giustiani who paid it 300 scudi[17]. The irony of fate has it that the brother of the Marquis, Benedetto, turned to Baglione, who for him will create the concurrent picture.

The Giustiniani family collection was also dispersed and sold, as happened to many famous and important collections. *Amor vincit omnia* was purchased by the Kaiser Friedrich Museum in Berlin; that's why it is located in Teutonic territory today.

We should not forget that during the trial the picture was defined

amor terreno[18]

a not negligible aspect.

In a non-place, a salient feature of Caravaggio's work, we find the figure of a young naked Cupid. The setting can easily be defined as a non-place because the painter undertakes to remove all possible spatial and temporal connotations from the scene: it is not clear if it is a scene in night-time, in daytime or in an intermediate phase and it is not even well defined if it is an interior or an exterior.

---

[17] Ancient Italian coin

[18] Ancient Italian words for "earthly love"

What is certain is that Cupid shares the stage of the painting with the inevitable light that expertly illuminates and creates photographic depth and roundness.

The most intense interpretation of the Milanese master's work is poetic: Cupid, with his arrows, manages to win against any Art (represented by musical instruments and geometric calculation) and any form of human power (armour and crown).

The technique used to paint the wings is incredible. The feathers have a consistency that reaches hyperrealism and the feathers do not envy the softness of the real ones.

Cupid's body looks like real flesh, the roundness created by the light and the folds due to the position of the body want to suggest us - and they really do very well - that we are facing a real person, in flesh and blood, and not an idea.

Cupid's gaze is that of a boy who is self-confident and aware of what he can represent for the painter.

We also know the name of this young model: Francesco Boneri.

He was the only one who play the role of Cupid for Caravaggio.

The traveller and critic Richard Symons talks about him in his *Diary* written in 1650, in his book he presents information that he collected during a trip to Italy. Symons, in addition to reporting that Caravaggio had painted the boy in several paintings also says that

he was her boyfriend

and he reaffirms the concept after few sentences remembering that

ye body and face of his (Caravaggio's) owne boy or servant thait (sic) laid with him.

The English critic never had the opportunity to speak with the person concerned, obviously, so he limited himself to gathering rumours about the country.

Many want to see in the character of Cupid, however, one of Caravaggio's pupils who simply lent himself for the pose.

However, some documents may confirm what Symons said in his diary. In fact, the cohabitation between the Milanese master and his servant-pupil is confirmed in a parish census of 1605 in which it is possible to read that the two shared a room.

Many English experts, including the eminent Freelberg, support and defend the thesis that Caravaggio had a relationship with the young Checco (as they called him in town).

Italian critics, especially those from the most Catholic area, have always rejected this possibility that borders on homoeroticism and want to see in Cupid a symbol of resurrection, victory and triumph.

Now, it being understood, that legally judging Caravaggio today for his relationship with a young boy does not make much sense; as it is nonsense to judge the Greco-Roman world for its ancient habit (so what should we say about Hadrian and his beloved Antinous?); we must be clear with ourselves and decide on how to consider this work.

Giving *Amor vincit omnia* a Christian or homoerotic key of reading - which reaches paedophilia - should depend solely and exclusively on the sensitivity of the viewer. Each of us can and should look at the picture with a personal predisposition and read it according to his own thought.

And as such it must be presented though.

The personal interpretation and the feelings aroused by the works should never be passed off as those of the artist but it must always be remembered that they belong to us and as such have never to be imposed on others as if they were absolute truth.

It would be like wanting everyone to conform to a single thought; how boring!

Honestly, I believe that knowing the true key to understanding a work of Art is not so indispensable for the purpose of viewing and enjoying a painting.

Returning to our work. If we try to read it in a homoerotic way first and more "Catholic" later, we will notice that in neither case the work loses its glamour, its beauty and its identity.

Since Art does not necessarily have to be moral, it is not fair to judge it according to ethics and morality. It must be lived for what it is, in total freedom of thought.

The morality and ethics that belong to our life will not fail due to a painting. We must also remember that these two important components of human mentality change over the centuries and it is not always possible to judge the past without taking into consideration these epochal changes in the thinking of society.

However, a tragic tale can be read in this fascinating work.

Everything we can accomplish in our lives is fleeting and destined to crumble. Arts, buildings, war and empires will remain lifeless and substance at the foot of a true and eternal being like *Love*.

Scene VI:
Squaring the circle

Even today, one of the most curious aspects of Caravaggio's Art is that of the interpretation and explanation of his works.

Today Art pushes us not to have to understand the canvas at all costs but to feel it and perceive its strength. In classical times, however, Art was the servant of the prevailing ideology both from a political and religious point of view (and too often, let us not forget that the two aspects coincided).

Art has been the preferred communication channel of power for many centuries, it is normal that we still try to read it according to the old school and we do not let ourselves be carried away by the sensations that are aroused. It matters little if they are not the author's own. When true, Art wants to be universal and therefore is open to different interpretations, of course.

Interpreting the pictorial choices of Caravaggio is not impossible but it is extremely difficult. Being basically a bad boy of painting, he never bothered to write his thoughts and the motivations of his artistic expression, which today would have been essential to be able to read some of his works.

Caravaggio is among the first painters to highlight the artist's presence in the works. The public, that of his years but also ours, should begin to observe his works, remembering that there was an artist behind the brush. And that this artist wanted to leave us his vision of the world.

One of the major constraints, in my opinion, suffered by one of his works concerns the famous *Basket of Fruit*.

A still life like many others, if we want, but with truly unique innovative aspects in the History of Art.

We are perhaps faced with one of the first metaphysical works of painting. The basket is located in a non-place; it is not possible to say for sure where we are: a cellar, a kitchen, outdoors or in a bright room? We are in a situation where time does not exist: the light that illuminates the basket is uniform, almost as if it came from a reflector, and it is not easy to say what time of day you are.

These two characteristics make the work universal; it is fine for any place and time. The work should be lived without any prejudice linked to two of the salient conditions of human finiteness: where and when. We are faced with a universal work and as such must be lived.

If possible, for Music lovers, it should be listened to as if it were a Bach fugue.

The Music of the great German master, one of the great fathers of Music, was written for Music itself. It does not have a real concept to express, it does not have an ideology to support. It is a Music to listen to, to appreciate for how it looks and how we perceive it and nothing else.

With the same conception we have just applied to Bach's Music, we should now observe the *Basket of Fruit*. It has nothing to say except its own Beauty. Beautiful, almost photographic, incredible; I believe it is already an unparalleled value.

The basket gives the idea of being real, you have the feeling of being able to grab and lift it from the shelf on which it rests. All this is due to the stroke of genius that Caravaggio had in painting the base of the basket not perfectly resting on the shelf. A part, the one towards us, leaves the edge of the shelf for a few centimetres, reproducing reality in an impressive way. On the other hand, not all shelves have been designed to be able to perfectly support a basket.

We have the difficult task of staying in front of the greatness of the work and observing it, whether to do it in silence or not is up to us to decide.

The true interpretation of the work, as long as it exists, is that present in the painter's head (if the author had had a precise idea by painting it!). If by observing a work we feel sensations that give us ideas and suggestions that can then lead to possible interpretations of the work, we must always and only remember that those will always be our personal ideas only.

It seems a simple concept and maybe even a foregone conclusion. Yet it is not always easy to avoid putting our words into the mouth of an artist.

Even the most distinguished Art experts can exaggerate a little too much with the interpretation.

A well-known writer, journalist and Art and architecture critic from the columns of a national newspaper has attributed even a Christological meaning to the *Basket of Fruit*. Incredibly, who signs the article recognizes Christ himself in the basket.

This interpretation is given by the fact that in the Sixteenth Century, the Eucharist was considered *"Charitas"* and *"Fructus*[19]*"*. Indeed, according to the Council of Trent, Christ is the Fruit of God given to men through the sacrament of the Eucharist.

The rule, and here we should not consider it a possibility, to read Caravaggio's work is to use the preaching of time as a basic grammar; in particular, we refer to the preaching of St. Charles Borromeo on 12th June 1583:

> *ciò che per primitiva Chiesa era Cristo è per noi l'Eucarestia; anzi la sua forza è la medesima, e voi ricevereste gli stessi frutti.*[20]

Personally, I consider it an excessive forcing.

---

[19] Latin words for "Charity" and "Fruit"

[20] "what was the primitive Church of Christ is the Eucharist for us; indeed, its strength is the same, and you would receive the same fruits"

We should not exclude, however, that we are faced with a possible interpretation and for those with particular religious needs it is also plausible; letting her pass through the thought of Caravaggio seems a little risky, as well as incorrect. A similar interpretation is also offered for *The Lute Player* kept in the opulent rooms of the Hermitage.

According to a very risky reading, the young musician should be understood as the groom of the Song of Songs.

So much purity and poetry are undoubtedly curious; especially if we think about the fact that we are talking about the artist who has decided to reproduce the funeral of a prostitute making it become that of the mother of Christ, who among many features has virginity unlike a prostitute.

If we continue to give space to these forced interpretations, we run the risk of creating a case similar to the denaturalization suffered by *The Return of the Prodigal Son* by Rubens. According to an interpretation, obviously a partisan one, they want to see in the father's hands those of a God who is both mother and father (in fact one hand is more defined and tapered while the other is larger and rough); what does not take this interpretation of the work into consideration is that the painter most likely made his hands that way because of an eye problem that did not allow him to focus well on the depth.

The public, more or less erudite and authoritative, has every right to experience Art by following its sensitivity; without forgetting to point out that it is one's own thought and not that of its creator.

The *Basket of Fruit* is a beautiful still life with a strong innovative character, and as such should be read and experienced. All the rest are only pleasant mental and cultural reflections that it is right to disclose with respect, also because they can undoubtedly enrich the public but do not add or take away anything significant from the work.

One of the greatest needs of humanity is to understand anything and to reduce it as much as possible to easily understandable. So, a bit like playing with the clouds when you want to see images that do not really exist, we apply the same rules to Art.

It seems that if we cannot have a logical explanation, we are prepared to invent it out of nothing.

If something does not make sense or why, it does not seem to have any value either. In Art this rule does not apply, not that it should be so in Life.

Everything becomes lawful in order to have a meaning.

Many have come to the point of being convinced that their personal interpretation is the absolute Truth, unfortunately, and these ideas are hidden in the folds of historical reality and it is increasingly difficult to recognize them.

Interpretation is not an absolute value in general but it is a personal truth and should remain so as such. Let us not forget that only works with multiple possible and logical interpretations are true works of Art.

Scene VII:
The influence of power

Many of Caravaggio's works have the audacity to present themselves as an outcry against Power, understood in all its forms and facets. Yet, however much you try to fight the established Power, to resize it in some way and to ridicule it, it is difficult to escape its perennial thirst for revenge against those who, somehow, try to oppose it.

However, protected, Caravaggio was also engulfed by the same monster he tried to destroy.

The relationship between Art and Power is much closer and more intimate than we are actually willing to accept at times. In a more classical period of the Arts, the influence of religion was vital not only for commissions but also for the presence on the market. The vast majority of requests for works of Art, in fact, were religious and the artists (who mostly fulfilled the role of highly specialized workers) simply had to use their learned artistic technique and their own pictorial language (properly called style) to tell stories from the Bible or a saints' biography.

In the case of political power, however, the painter - even in this case - was not asked to think much, he could not worry about expressing his ethics or his vision of the world but he had to devote himself to a much simpler practice (if I can afford, perhaps even more superficially): idealize the representative of the Power or the State.

At the beginning, when it began to take its first steps, Art mainly fulfilled its apotropaic function par excellence: to be a good omen for hunting and survival, as well as the need to be able to demonstrate one's existence beyond space and time. In this regard, the hand made on the wall of a cave is truly moving, as if to say: "I was there and it was me". Some habits have remained unchanged throughout human history, one of them is raising your open hand to let them know you are there, as during the appeal at school.

At some point in history, Art becomes a profession and allows artists to get paid for their work. We are still far from the economic independence of artists which is a characteristic of our days. The financial resources to pay for the realization of the works and to keep the artist himself were the peculiarity of a few subjects in the society of the time. Thus, the major commissions were of religious nature - the Vatican and its major representatives have always enjoyed substantial economic means - or political background (with special regard to monarchy and its various major or minor representatives).

The artist's life was not overly complicated from a concept point of view; once a good technical skill was acquired and the right symbols were known to be inserted to facilitate the interpretation by an indoctrinated audience, the bulk of the work was already done. Whether it was eternal redemption or punishment, welfare or power of the State, everything had been codified and the symbols returned similar to themselves in the different works.

We have a first notice of change with the artist who perhaps less than anyone else in the Art scene was an innovator and created a rift with the past: Raphael.

Around 1513-1514 the master of Urbino made the Sistine Madonna, one of his absolute masterpieces now preserved at the Gemäldegalerie in Dresden. The famous painting became a myth for the public knowledge because of the famous detail of the pair of angels, somewhat bored and somewhat listless, which were reproduced with some frequency on clothing objects and boxes of chocolates.

This work, having removed the nice atmosphere of the little angels, who however say a lot about the spirit with which it was made, has a strongly irreverent character and is definitely outside the box.

If we start reading the work right from the couple of little angels, we can realize that they are on a stage. The arms of the little ones rest on the wooden boards of a stage. Raising our gaze towards the Holy Virgin, we meet an apparition that seems to respect all visual canons: the wind that inflates the veil, the cloud under the woman's feet and two saints on her sides.

Looking more closely, questions arise: why the stage? Why the stick probably made of slightly curved iron? Why the green curtain?

Could Raphael have been struck by an attack of rebellion or strong satire against that religion which has always been his best client?

One has the idea that Raphael almost wanted to suggest that all those beliefs about apparitions, assumptions and sacred conversations were not very different from a beautiful popular theatrical representation.

Was it the representation of the popular and jester criticism of the theatre companies that offered their sometimes-irreverent shows in the Italian squares or one of the first attempts by an artist to make his own personal thought known, which in this case is far from dictates of the religious institution?

In a very cynical way, let me tell you that the Raphael affair that could be created is not so interesting right now.

It is very interesting to tie this probable first attempt to show one's voice in a work that has also been accepted by the Power. But as always happens in Art History, Raphael was never the first to have had an idea.

If we go back in time fifty years (more precisely between 1460 and 1469), we meet Antonello da Messina who made his *Salting Madonna* now preserved at the National Gallery in London. A beautiful painting with a Nordic echo in which we can observe a Virgin holding her Son in her arms and two angels holding a beautiful Flemish-flavoured crown on the woman's head. Angels seem to want to reveal a secret. If we carefully observe their wings, we can see that they have no canonical characteristics. They seem to be fastened with pins, apparently, they have no feathers or feathers and they seem to be made of paper.

It almost seems that Antonello da Messina wants to suggest that angels are equipped with wings only for our representation needs. Their costumes look like theatrical ones created by a costume designer with little experience.

It is difficult not to think of being in front of an artistic dig taken at common thinking, which wants angels (spiritual beings) with wings (a physical and mechanical means) to be able to fly. Michelangelo (Buonarroti) also proposed the same thought in a more veiled way, actually he decided to represent angels in the act of flying and without wings.

Caravaggio has a more impetuous character and loves being irreverent; that's why prostitutes and lovers made as the only true, pure and sacred love.

His painting does not join the chorus, a constant warning to change the point of view and think with your own head, in a different way and not according to the rules established by others.

His strong character and his desire for fun pushed him to the brink of public insult. Power fascinates and bewitches, Caravaggio knew it very well being born in a wealthy society and being able to count very influential friendships. He loved the life in the palaces and willingly frequented the frescoed rooms and as a predictable scion of good society who perhaps out of boredom or the desire to assert an independent and free personality, began to denigrate and oppose a society that based all its conventions and rules on the teachings of Catholicism.

The story of Caravaggio reminds us of a simple fact: Power does not allow anyone to leave without paying a pledge.

Throughout his life, Power has been on the trail of Caravaggio, it has consumed him until his departure. Merisi's life was a continuous struggle against himself and against society and was theatrical and baroque until the end.

Scene VIII:
The Order of Caravaggio

If he had lived in our day, it is almost certain that Caravaggio would have been very sensitive to copyright and to the protection of the authorship of the work of Art.

His would not be simply a just and legitimate desire to protect his work and receive the compensation due (a dream unattainable even today for many artists!) but would be the outburst of jealousy he felt for his creations.

Usually, most artists, in order to guarantee a higher standard of living, very willingly opened a workshop. This allowed them to have a real income from the unskilled labour to which they taught the job; more or less like some training internships offered today to recent graduates who would like to start a career.

The workshops were lively and very interesting environments, where very young aspiring artists lived (sometimes the aspiration was more than the parents, however, let's face it) -in the most literal sense of the term- helping the master in the most practical and boring tasks such as the production of colour (when it was fine) or the cleanliness of the workshop itself. Working for the master, they could first learn the rudiments and then the subtleties of Painting until they were ready to face the world of Art on their own.

Sometimes it happened that the important name of the workshop could afford the luxury of accepting more commissions than those achievable, so much after the initial setting on his part of the work, it was completed by the best students.

Caravaggio, also in this respect, stroke a discordant note. He never opened his own workshop or wanted it; in part, the death sentence and consequently wandering life could not allow it. It is difficult to think that a man with a personality at the edge and against orthodoxy, could open a workshop and be a guide and reference point for young people who wanted to take this path. The Lombard master had hardly trained in a workshop and certainly did not want to relive that environment.

He had female and male models and young assistants - we have already talked about his assistant-lover in detail - but it all ended there. In his world was contemplated the presence of handsome people who animated his life but nothing more. His attitude has always been that of wanting to create a court of person dedicated to his well-being and his pleasure (not only sexual but also existential) and nothing more.

This reticence of his teaching and of giving birth to an artistic descent did not, however, hinder the formation of a group of followers who imbued themselves with his works and the atmospheres created by the master, even going so far as to consider himself a group of faithful followers: the Caravaggisti.

The ranks of people who have suffered a strong influence from the Art of Caravaggio directly or indirectly is somewhat impressive. This knowledge, albeit superficial of Caravaggio's artistic court, will reserve some surprises.

One of the best known names of his artistic followers is that of **Orazio Gentileschi**. Quite fascinating character for his questionable ethics. It is not difficult to remember the choice made by this gentleman to convince his daughter to get married. In this period, the female condition was far from enjoying the slightest social benefit. Since his daughter gave some problems in the choice of the future husband, the father in a very unromantic way (it would be nice to tell us about a chivalric adventure in which two suitors challenged each other in a single battle, but it was not so) he agreed with what he thought was the best party concerned and advised the bold young man in love to rape the girl. Agostino Tassi, this is the name of the man who committed the combined crime, was a painter esteemed above all by Orazio who believed he could find in him a trusted assistant as well as a caring son-in-law. This, unfortunately, was not the only evil done by this questionable father towards his daughter. Since not even with that rape she decided to get married, indeed the woman filed a lawsuit against the rapist and won but she never saw her tormentor serving the right sentence and even if she has absurdity she was publicly stigmatized by the society, Orazio eliminated her from his will, to then enter her name again among the beneficiaries following a manoeuvre designed to convince his daughter to collaborate with him. To convince her, he promised her a public apology, the payment of her honorarium and to return to being considered a dear daughter at the time of opening the will. Obviously, Artemisia worked for her painter father and then not only was she cancelled again from her paternal will but she was not even paid for her work. Orazio is undoubtedly a character with villainous characteristics, a little like Caravaggio, and his painting has undergone an even greater influence from the Milanese painter. What differentiates him from the Lombard master is the genius and artistic quality, a good painter Gentileschi but far from the uniqueness of Michelangelo Merisi and undoubtedly less gifted than his daughter.

A lot has been written about **Artemisia Gentileschi** and has fictionalized even more. Her paintings about *Judith and Holofernes* converse with the master's works as if they were old schoolmates, without that reverential fear that could arise from minor works towards those of the great artist. Artemisia is a woman who in life had to face very difficult moments and after her death her situation has not changed much. Her account of the rape she suffered is simply terrible:

Serrò la camera a chiave e dopo serrata mi buttò su la sponda del letto dandomi con una mano sul petto, mi mise un ginocchio fra le cosce ch'io non potessi serrarle et alzatomi li panni, che ci fece grandissima fatica per alzarmeli, mi mise una mano con un fazzoletto alla gola et alla bocca acciò non gridassi e le mani quali prima mi teneva con l'altra mano mi le lasciò, havendo esso prima messo tutti doi li ginocchi tra le mie gambe et appuntendomi il membro alla natura cominciò a spingere e lo mise dentro. E li sgraffignai il viso e li strappai li capelli et avanti che lo mettesse dentro anco gli detti una stretta al membro che gli ne levai anco un pezzo di carne»[21].

After this horrible crime she underwent a trial that saw her recognized in her role as a violated victim but which was in itself a small victory since society (the worst of the courts) gave more credit to the false hired testimonies. So, Artemisia in addition to undergoing a rape, in addition to having to testify without the time to overcome the psychological trauma (she had to tell over and over again what happened and also had to undergo numerous and humiliating gynaecological examinations) she also had to suffer the shame given to her by the society that wrote numerous sonnets denigrating her and defining her vulgarly

---

[21] "He locked the room and after being locked he threw me on the edge of the bed pushing me with a hand on the chest, he put a knee between my thighs so that I could not tighten them and after having got up my cloths, which he made a great effort to get up, put me a hand with a handkerchief at the throat and mouth so that I did not shout and the hands which before held me with the other hand left me, having first put all of them on my knees between my legs and pinning me his member to my vagina began to push and put it inside. And I scratched his face and pulled out his hair and before he put it inside I also gave him a squeeze on the member who also took off a piece of meat."

puttana bugiarda che va a letto con tutti[22].

Yet, this strong and unique woman, despite everything, led a life that to define modern is too little. She opens her workshop, keeps up with her work and leaves the house to shop when she needs it and goes alone to buy the colours to make her works. Needless to remind us that at that time, in Italy, this lifestyle was considered depraved. Artemisia will do more, as a good revolutionary who destabilizes the system (the similarity with Caravaggio is evident!) she will collect enough money to be able to guarantee the dowry to her daughters. All this obviously with the aggravating circumstance of a husband (in the meantime she had also married) who practiced the profession of painter without great success but was an excellent spendthrift.

After her death the struggles did not end. It will be a handful of women who wants to violate her in her intimacy and drama. In fact, with the advent of feminism they wanted to take our Artemisia as a fervent *ante litteram* feminist. This consideration (reckless, according to me) comes from a superficial reading of his works and his most frequent representation: Judith cuts off Holofernes' head, the woman takes revenge on the man.

This is, however, an extreme attempt to overcome the trauma that she has never had the chance to fully overcome.

---

[22] lying bitch who sleeps with everyone

Merisi's and Gentileschi's Art are deeply linked by the strong violent impact of both the scenes and the colours and also by the tendency to make everything theatrical and plausible. Let us not forget the strong character of both which is expressed without doubt through the painted scenes but also, and above all, by the awareness of themselves. Artemisia will create an allegory of Painting: a self-portrait of her while she is intent on painting, as if to say that she herself is painting. A self-confidence worthy of Caravaggio himself.

Despite this harsh biography, Artemisia has also found a way to have fun and be herself. According to recent studies, she too liked nightlife very much and spent her evenings in taverns, where she never held back if there was fun.

Another painter who suffered the strong influence of Michelangelo was **Francesco Boneri**, called Cecco di Caravaggio. He himself, the helper-lover who was often portrayed by the Milanese master as his favourite model and to whom he attributed the characteristics of *Amor vincit omnia*. From the nickname given to him it is easy to understand that that belonging to Caravaggio has been very strong, on the other hand we have already talked about their relationship.

The most curious of all his disciples (albeit indirectly) was **Giovanni Baglione**. Just him, that Baglione who was the target of many teasing (very heavy and slanderous) by Caravaggio himself. Guilty of having been inspired so much by the Art of his Lombard friend to be accused by him of plagiarism. A friendship without a shadow of a doubt not very boring that between the two: admiration by Baglione, slanderous derision by Caravaggio; not exactly the best conditions for a long and healthy friendship.

Bartolomeo Manfredi from the Cremona area (to be precise from Ostiano) wins the prize for most intense among the Caravaggisti. Despite his strong pictorial charge, however, he has been penalized by history and is almost unknown today. This poor critical fortune of his is mainly due to the rumour that had been circulated about him according to which he was a forger and created works with the intent of selling them as if they were by Caravaggio. Obviously, this is what happens to those who put too little of themselves into artistic creation. A true artist is the one who manages to become immortal and to do this one must instil the vision that characterizes his life into his Art. Copying from other people's works requires a good dose of technique and ability but it is not the most incisive choice and you are forgotten, as it should be.

The painter of Italian-Swiss origin ***Giovanni Serodine*** trained on the study and observation of Caravaggio's works. With the achievement of his artistic maturity he will even go so far as to push the drama of his canvases to the point of becoming almost visionary.

In the Genoa area we find ***Domenico Fiasella***, ***Gioacchino Assereto***, ***Orazio De Ferrari***.

While in Naples we should not forget ***Battistello Caracciolo*** and ***Carlo Sellitto***.

Rome at this time was an important centre not only for the training of new generations of artists but was also the most living centre of the Art market.

One of the greatest aspirations for most artists was to move to Rome. Among the communities of foreign artists present in the eternal city we find that of the Dutch. Among them there are many Caravaggisti like ***Hendrick ter Brugghen*** and ***Gerrit*** *van Honthorst*. The latter after his apprenticeship in Italy even obtained the patronage of Charles I Stuart. He was a very prolific painter and left us an impressive number of works but those that had the greatest public success were those that showed a greater influence by Caravaggio. Suffice it to say that it was precisely because of his scenes often represented in taverns, with musicians, gamblers or simple people intent on eating that he went down in history as *Gerrit delle notti*[23]. He learned so well the chiaroscuro technique indirectly taught to him by Caravaggio that he often offered us scenes lit simply by a single candle, thus giving us suggestions that not only did justice to his skill and his artistic name but also to all the inspiration infused by the work of Michelangelo Merisi.

Even among French painters someone was enchanted by Caravaggio's grammar.

Among the most important French painters who have undergone a strong influence of the Lombard master there are names of all respect: **Louis Le Nain**, **Valentin de Boulogne**, **Simon Vouet**. Names that unfortunately do not say much to the general public, because they are unjustly considered not so unique by the curators and critics.

Among the best-known painters in that time in France we have **Georges de La Tour**; born in a wealthy family (a bit like our Caravaggio) he completes his training trip to Rome and here he also discovers the world of light and shadow of the Milanese master. The passion he feels for this pictorial style will lead him to be an important representative of the Baroque

---

[23] Gerrit of the nights

Art in his country, gathering so much consensus that it becomes nothing less than

ordinary painter of the King.

Despite the strong influence felt by Georges de La Tour for the works of Caravaggio, he does not limit himself to following the style of the master (as many have done) but impresses his personal vision on the Caravaggio's world of chiaroscuro so much that it is possible today to compare them as two elements at the antipodes. Very interesting in this regard is the thought of the French writer André Malraux according to which Georges de La Tour as opposed to Caravaggio

he interpreted the serene part of the darkness.

Malraux praises the compatriot by writing that

it took his genius to conceive a transparent Caravaggio.

Looking closely at the works of Georges de La Tour, however, we also realize another factor: the French painter, of course, creates so serene and transparent works strongly influenced by Caravaggio but he is unable to give flesh and blood to his figures, which remain rigid and pleasantly

Northern European. Perhaps the strong points identified by Malraux proved to be a double-edged sword that turned against its owner; if de La Tour had been a little less serene it would have offered some more emotion. One aspect that unites him to all his Caravaggisti colleagues is that of the use of candlelight that illuminates the darkness; the candle represents the limit that the Caravaggisti have not exceeded, in fact, Caravaggio did not need a source of light to justify the well-studied and intelligent brightness of his works, for him light was a protagonist of the work and not an effect originated from a source. Merisi dared more, giving an almost human value to this presence while for all the others it was a complement (albeit important) of the scenography.

Spain deserves a separate discussion, since the conditioning of the Art of Caravaggio did not affect ordinary artists, but the founding fathers of Spanish Art.

Among the artistic personalities influenced by Caravaggio we find those who not only represent the history of Spanish Painting but who, for centuries, have been the masters of generations of painters: **Francisco de Zurbarán, Bartolomé Esteban Murillo** and **Diego Velázquez**.

A special mention deserves an Italian by adoption such as **Jusepe de Ribera**, called Lo Spagnoletto[24]. Born in Spain, of course, he decided to move to Naples where he remained until the end of his life. He played the role of big protagonist in Neapolitan Art and we find him in the company of names such as Luca Giordano, Mattia Preti and Salvator Rosa. His painting

---

[24] The Little Spaniard

is strongly characterized by the late style of Caravaggio, which historians have been labelled with the name of "tenebrism", which, as the name implies, is characterized by particularly dark and gloomy atmospheres.

After a long period of oblivion, Caravaggio returned to give painting lessons and among the students sitting on the desks of his school we find **Jacques-Louis David**, **Francisco Goya**, **Théodore Géricault**, **Eugène Delacroix** and **Gustave Courbet**.

All this can only make us reflect on the importance and strength of the Painting of Michelangelo Merisi, who with his works has influenced (and continues to influence) European Painting.

BACKSTAGE

Scene I:
The designer

Among the many works by the Lombard master, there is a very nice one; not so much for the scene told as for the choice of our painter, who led him to explore a modern area so that he can easily be considered our contemporary.

Walking through the rooms of the Uffizi in Florence, at a certain point we are welcomed into a room of modest dimensions by a screaming lady. It is one of the most incisive works in the history of Italian Art.

Medusa watches us with her eyes and mouth wide open in a deafening silent scream. After the initial bewilderment given by such fatal beauty, turning around the glass case that houses this marvel, we realize that the work is not a real painting but a shield decorated by Caravaggio's brush.

The choice of the support is decidedly unusual but since it is a work by Caravaggio, we cannot expect too much normality.

Obviously, it was not so unusual to decorate the shields, in the ethnographic and archaeological museums we can admire incredible wonders made in every moment of human history. The parade armours, those that were used in ceremonies, were accompanied by swords or shields that are real works of Art.

One wonders if this is also the case with Caravaggio's shield.

In 2002 the restoration was completed following the cowardly attack on Via dei Georgofili in 1993[25]. The work suffered minimal damage but as it was in a difficult state of conservation it was decided to restore it (conducted by Stefano Scarpelli and Caterina Caneva) following which it was confirmed its classification among the parade shields typical of the Sixteenth Century and in particular it would have been made for the armoury of Ferdinando I de' Medici.

Obviously, everything is possible and everything is probable until any next denials, on the other hand it is perfectly known that Science is always ready to update itself.

However, care must be taken not to lose sight of the main aspect of this unique masterpiece.

---

[25] The Italian mafia blew up a car packed with explosives in a street in Florence near the Uffizi, causing several deaths and ruining the museum's works of Art.

Usually, the metal or painted decorations that can be admired on the shields performed the function of decorating the object, becoming an added value.

An extraordinary event happens in Caravaggio's *Medusa*: the object disappears in favour of the decoration, so much so that for most people that it is a shield, it could be a discovery.

Decorating armours and shields with the face of Medusa is a practice that takes us back to the Roman era; before them we find the Etruscans, who giving it a strong apotropaic value used her image as decoration of the antefixes (that is, the covers that were placed on the head of the roof beams or as occlusion of the terminal channels of the tiles).

All these objects are always perceived for their function and they are given the right added value due to the decoration created. For Caravaggio's *Medusa* this does not happen easily.

With a little courage and a healthy dose of ruthlessness, Caravaggio could be called one of the first designers in history.

The phenomenon of design belongs mainly to our time since it is strongly connected to industrial production. With the mass production that allows a reduction in construction costs and consequently a lower purchase price, the first characteristic of today to be sacrificed was Beauty, which is known, increases production costs exponentially.

In order for an object not to be simply functional but to have the right dose of Beauty (which does not add anything to functionality, but makes you live better), you had to turn to very specialized workers who, with a massive use of time, means and knowledge, created unique objects that few could afford.

With the flourishing of the industry, a lot of beauty was wasted but at some point, someone opposed to this trend. Thus, was born the team of designers, people engaged in the daily struggle in favour of Beauty (sometimes uncomfortable and difficult to use, but so beautiful).

Since prehistoric times, humans have spent time and energy decorating everyday objects, transforming what could be banal and useful into something beautiful, useful and refined. Although with different means and results, this also continues between the productions of large-scale mass distribution, where Beauty is perhaps reduced to the bone but still tries to point out its pale presence.

The designer's work is successful when an object retains its function, remains recognizable but acquires a unique Beauty that perhaps did not belong to it before.

With his *Medusa*, Caravaggio has all the credentials to be considered a *star designer*.

The intensity that he reaches with his brush in creating the severed head of the gorgon is such as not to make us even perceive the banality of the decorated object. We are faced with a simple wooden round shield: nothing exceptional, if we just observe the object. A banal support, if we like, for a work that has become one of the most famous and recognized all around the world.

This work represents a turning point in the History of Art, precisely because of the perceptual impact it still arouses in the public.

Caravaggio was the first great artist to make his Art at disposal for the decoration of objects, highlighting beauty so much that the object disappeared; a trend so modern that we can easily find ourselves in it today.

Perhaps a question may have arisen for some of us while visiting a design exhibition or gallery: what is the object I am seeing for?

This happens because the search for Beauty (which is sometimes so subjective as to be incomprehensible) has gone so far as to minimize the usefulness of an object. We should be careful though; this phenomenon does not have to be considered negative. In itself, every object (even the most banal) is chosen for its shape or colour (in a nutshell, as far as it can be beautiful) and the human being always tries to surround himself with as much beauty as possible.

Caravaggio can safely be considered as the father of modern design just to make us forget the round shield in favour of his Medusa head.

Obviously, Michelangelo Merisi did not have the slightest intention of sowing a seed that would bear fruit a few centuries later. Any subsequent consideration of this event must - for intellectual honesty - always consider the arbitrariness of the artists' choices. In my opinion, an unforgivable mistake is not made if we place Caravaggio among the most successful designers who have sublimated, thanks to their work, the human need for Beauty, which is the ultimate goal of design.

Not shocking with particularly incredible or out of the ordinary creations but delighting everyday life (which, unfortunately for us, is often trivial) with an extraordinary beauty.

Scene II:
The Art of capriccio

Art spends most of its existence in an attempt not to suffocate among the needs of the powers that require its work.

There is no artist who is completely free to express himself without any kind of influence from the market, religion or political power. Absolute independence from this (sometimes diabolical) triad could be the cause of the total invisibility of that artist who decides to live his Art without getting involved in these strong powers. Unfortunately, we know it well, skill and genius are not enough to be successful in life, you always need a bit of luck and the right contacts.

Simply: either you accept the rules or you are not even in the least considered.

Over the centuries, we have had artists who have been able to extricate themselves in a brilliant way between the demands of power and the need to express themselves. Someone has developed two lines of artistic production (one that winks at power and a more intimate and personal one), someone else has hidden details in the works in the hope that someone in the audience will notice and codify them; others worked hard to be able to achieve economic security such that they could then feel free to do what they most wanted to do, regardless of the commissions and ideas of the clients.

Our Caravaggio has very often inserted in works commissioned to him details (sometimes not so hidden) that reveal his thoughts or even just simply the desire to make fun of the public or clients.

We have already understood that the Milanese master was an extreme character in his choices. But we cannot fail to do justice to his unparalleled craftsmanship and his choices in the artistic field. For Merisi, the work of Art must continue to be created with particular attention to commissions and the market, because they remain the only possible channel to be able to support himself through Art. Freelance in the artistic field will begin to be a possibility only a couple of centuries later, an era in which our old Europe is travelled far and wide by Wolfgang Amadeus Mozart.

Despite this attention towards the clients, obviously completely interested, Caravaggio has never lost the opportunity to be able to tell his vision of reality, obviously always and only in strong colours.

Unknowingly, Michelangelo Merisi indicated a completely new direction for Art and this opportunity will be seized over a century later by the famous Spanish painter Francisco José de Goya y Lucientes, known to all simply as Francisco Goya.

Despite the important difference of time between the two masters, the closeness of their Art is impressive and it even seems that Goya takes Caravaggio's palette as an example to create his own. Brown and black colours are so similar that they can have a real dialogue despite the unbridgeable space-time distance.

The eighty plates by Goya, who without a shadow of a doubt can be considered one of the fathers of Spanish Painting, and which go under the title of *Caprichos* are a successful attempt to highlight the vices, baseness and aberrations of society.

The Spanish painter plays the difficult and dangerous role of objective portraitist of reality without giving any discounts to anyone, suffice it to recall the portraits of the royal family where the king and the queen with not exactly beautiful faces and not very smart expressions are surrounded by equally questionable characters.

The *Capriccio* in itself is a highly free form of Art, which arises from the author's need to feel free of constraints in the stylistic choice and content of his work. This kind of artistic realization has a purely personal value since it is not born to meet the favours of a specific client. The artist exhibits his feelings and thoughts or considerations in total freedom and this, with great surprise at the time, could still meet the public's favour. Because we know, the personal thoughts of each of us can be shared by many.

Despite this important similarity between the two painters, their Art is dedicated to the *capriccio* in a different way.

Caravaggio turned his attention to the more spiritual aspect of existence by teasing the public on purely religious and moral issues; most of the sharp "judgments" expressed in his painting turn to the dogmas imposed by religion, and to the desire to amaze at all costs by going against the common thinking.

For Goya, the object of his *capriccios* is essentially the society made up of questionable human beings, sometimes narrow-minded and not really enlightened by reason.

His works can be read as real satirical attacks on that society that the artist not only could not fully understand but considered filled with ugliness.

Just as Caravaggio has never tried to veil the sarcastic and provocative references in his works, Goya too has underlined in all possible ways the true meanings of his plates, even if (anticipating the films and television series that are the rage today) he wanted to point out that everything came out from his imagination.

Poiché la maggior parte delle cose rappresentate in quest'opera è di natura mentale, non sarà temerario credere che gli intenditori scuseranno forse le loro mancanze, tanto più che l'autore non ha seguito esempi altrui, né ha potuto copiare la natura. E se l'imitazione

> *della natura è già abbastanza difficile e ammirevole quando riesce, guadagnerà certo un po' di stima anche colui che, allontanandosi del tutto da essa, fu costretto a esibire forme che fino a quel momento esistevano solo nello spirito umano, oscurato e confuso dalla mancanza di rischiaramento o surriscaldato dalla sfrenatezza delle passioni*[26].

Yet something is not right in this extreme attempt not to be excessively harassed by the authorities in office at the time, among which we cannot forget the Holy Inquisition (even if it had very little of holy). Characters with easily recognizable names and surnames were hidden among the caricatures and faces depicted.

Charles Baudelaire himself wrote

> *Frati che sbadigliano, frati che gozzovigliano, facce squadrate di assassini che si preparano a mattutino, facce astute, ipocrite, aguzze e malvagie come profili di uccelli rapaci [...] streghe, sabba, diavolerie, bambini arrostiti allo spiedo, che so? Tutte le dissolutezze del sogno, tutte le iperboli dell'allucinazione, e poi tutte quelle spagnole*

---

[26] Since most of the things represented in this work are of a mental nature, it will not be foolhardy to believe that connoisseurs will perhaps excuse their shortcomings, especially since the author has not followed others' examples, nor has he been able to copy Nature. And if the imitation of Nature is already difficult and admirable enough when it succeeds, even the one who, completely moving away from it, was forced to exhibit forms that until that moment existed only in the human spirit, obscured, will certainly gain some esteem. and confused by the lack of enlightenment or overheated by the wildness of the passions.

bianche e slanciate che certe vecchie perpetue lavano e preparano per il sabba, o per la prostituzione della sera, il sabba della nostra civiltà![27]

Caravaggio and Goya share a vision that will lead Art to be what we know today: not at the service of the client but a channel for the transmission of thought and ideas.

The *capriccio* will become more and more present in Art, until it is completely purified, becoming free from the pressures of the ideologies of various commissions.

To obtain its freedom from the power constituted by politics, aristocracy and religion, Art had to pay a high price and compromise with the devil: market.

This phenomenon is under our eyes, every day. Power is now concentrated in the hands of the market which determines not only the value of goods and money but also the value of artistic creation and of human beings.

---

[27] Friars yawning, friars revelling, square faces of murderers preparing for matins, cunning, hypocritical, sharp and evil faces like profiles of birds of prey [...] witches, sabbaths, devilry, children roasted on a spit, what do I know? All the debauchery of the dream, all the hyperbole of hallucination, and then all the slender white Spanish ladies that certain old priest's housekeeper wash and prepare for the sabbath, or for the prostitution of the evening, the sabbath of our civilization!

Scene III:
The influence of Borromeo

Despite the need for freedom of expression and criticism that has always been invoked by works of Art, there is always a need for a charismatic figure to launch a fashion or an artist. Today this task is up to the communicators and Art critics (even if at times they seem to be sellers, rather than real critics), who have put their critical sense to sleep in favour of the economic sensitivity that develops with the percentages linked to sales of the works they sponsor.

At the time of Michelangelo Merisi (and for a few more centuries) the most important influencers were the high prelates of Roman Catholic Church, who were often more active in the secular world than to the spiritual one.

Among these, the figure of a Milanese cardinal stands out, Federico Borromeo, cousin of the much better-known Charles Borromeo, an important and very nice figure of the Milanese church.

Out of respect for the hierarchical rank reached and for simpler seniority, we start from Saint Charles.

Despite his sanctification, Borromeo was a curious character, more suited to a film or theatrical script than to a hagiographic tale.

Born in Arona, on what is now the Piedmonts shore of Lake Maggiore, he is without a doubt the most famous character of the noble Milanese family who still resides in the Lombard capital.

For a certain period of time he was a contemporary of Caravaggio (born in 1571) since he died on 3rd November 1584.

Without a doubt, being Borromeo one of the great reformers of the Catholic Church (together with St. Ignatius of Loyola and St. Philip Neri), Caravaggio's Art will draw great inspiration from the changes implemented by St. Charles.

Obviously, the full development of Borromeo's counter-reformist ideas took place during the full maturity of Caravaggio who absorbed many ideas. The thought of St. Charles was not only addressed to theological and ideological aspects but also to those of a social and cultural nature. His brotherly and protective love for his sisters was so strong that it only matched his misogynistic sentiment.

He did not have a very positive opinion of women; indeed, it can be said that his vision of the female world was very bad. To be fair, only two categories of women were able to enjoy the admiration of St. Charles Borromeo: his sisters and the women locked up in convents. I know it is not much but it is always better than nothing, as they say.

If we then think that one of his greatest merit was that of never having addressed a word to a woman, the circle closes with a nice coup de theatre.

Much has been said about this wave of misogyny propagated by Borromeo's ideas, some information is the result of pure fantasy while others are historically accepted and founded.

We have also waited to purge the valley[28] from witches which was almost all infested with this plague with the perdition of many souls, among which many had received mercifully in penance with abjuration, some given to the secular court as unrepentant with public execution of justice.

These words were addressed on 9th December 1583 by Borromeo to Cardinal Paleotti. During the visit to Val Mesolcina, 162 trials were recorded and 12 ended with a death sentence for the accused, only one of them was a man

---

[28] The valley to which we refer is the Val Mesolcina (in the Italian part of Switzerland), which Borromeo visited when he wrote this letter.

(moreover he was no less than the provost of the Collegiate church of San Vittore). These executions were conducted in the most impressive way possible (the condemned were burned alive and upside down) using the terror technique; the more the people were shocked, the less they would try to rebel against the new visions of reality. Without considering that, however, both in that period and today, the morbid taste for violence and pain of others has always been well rooted in most of the population.

However, it is well known that humanity is able to climb the highest peaks of Beauty but also to descend into the abysses of the worst atrocities.

In this atmosphere of continuous threats and tensions, not only did our Caravaggio live but also suffered the shame of the death sentence. The theme of condemnation and morbidity is often present in Caravaggio's Painting. In addition, there seems to be a strange link between the Caravaggio's Virgins and the prevailing idea of women at the time.

The fact that most of the Virgins are recognized prostitutes (and also recognizable to the people of the time) can be a very strong reminder of the thought of the time that saw in every woman the origin of evil and perdition. Obviously, in addition to the irreverence that always characterizes Merisi's works.

Another crusade supported by Borromeo was the one against fun and celebration, so much so that he wanted to ban and outlaw almost any occasion of celebration, together with male and female fashion that could be a cause of perdition and a possible erotic appeal. So, just to please, in addition to banning the holidays, they have banned also pomp and above all colours, in favour of a much soberer black.

Black everywhere and for anyone, obviously also for Art.

As a response from Art, which is always attentive to changes in society, colours seem to disappear from almost all fashionable palettes and black takes over all the possible space of the canvases.

Caravaggio is the greatest master of the use of black and will teach most of his fellow painters. Among colours it is the one that most conveys mystery, elegance (remember Chanel) and let us not forget that it creates a unique play with light giving an incredible thickness and relief to the figures.

Yet in this case it also conveys a slight echo of sadness; colours were banned to convey a sense of sadness that had to punish habits considered too festive and frivolous.

Another Borromeo also had a very strong influence on Caravaggio's life: Federico Borromeo, cousin of St. Charles. Much has been said about him, especially by Manzoni, who wanted him to be among the most prominent and important characters of his *The Betrothed*.

He was rare men at any time, who employed an excellent ingenuity, all the means of a great opulence, all the advantages of a privileged condition, a continuous intent, in seeking and exercising the best.

The description taken from Manzoni's best-known work has some truth. In fact, together with his cousin, Federico was one of the greatest cultural reformers in northern Italy (just think that in the colossus of Arona, St. Charles is represented with a book in his hand).

His commitment to spreading culture led him to open the Biblioteca Ambrosiana in 1607, as Manzoni also recalls in the XXII chapter of his work, where we can read that

> *this Biblioteca Ambrosiana that Federigo conceived with such spirited brilliance and he erected, with so much effort, from the foundations.*

It is nice to think that, today, the famous *Basket of Fruit* that decreed the start of Michelangelo Merisi's career is located right at the Ambrosiana, the home of Federigo Borromeo who bought it during his stay in Rome at the Cardinal Del Monte palace.

The first document certifying Borromeo's ownership of the painting dates back to 17th September 1607:

> *Un quadro di lunghezza un braccio, et di tre quarti all'incirca di altezza, dove in campo bianco è dipinto un Canestro di frutti parte ne rami con lor foglie, et parte spiccati da essi*
> *fra questi vi sono due grappoli d'uva, uno di bianca et*

l'altro di nera, fichi, mele, et altri di mano di Michele Agnolo da Caravaggio[29].

The bond that exists among the two high Milanese prelates and their native painter is very close and involves not only the historical and personal aspect but also, and above all, cultural formation.

---

[29] A picture of one arm in length, and approximately three quarters in height, where on a white field a Basket of fruits is painted, part of the branches with their leaves, and part of them stand out/among these there are two bunches of grapes, one white and/the other in black, figs, apples, and others by hand of Michele Agnolo [ancient form for Michelangelo] from Caravaggio.

Scene IV:
Scandal!

O nce, always at the time when Caravaggio walked the scenes of the artistic stage together with the Carraccis, Guido Reni, Domenichino and Guercino, the famous Giambattista Marino wrote

The poet's aim is wonder
(I'm talking about the excellent and not the clumsy):

> *who does not know how to surprise, should dedicate himself to the currycomb!*

Marino had already understood that Poetry (and in general we can extend the whole discussion to Art) does not necessarily have to devote itself to Beauty, a concept as fickle as it is not very definable, but it must amaze.

The amazement must pass through the refinement and beauty of the shapes, the refined technique and the harmony of the shapes. The *clumsiness* is unlikely to arouse astonishment, it is more likely to be a source of criticism and confirmation of the lack of even a minimal technical learned.

Apart from the clumsy attempts to create Art, which are usually made by neophytes or by unprepared and improvised artists, the wonder remains; before continuing, let the dictionary help us with the definition of this fascinating word:

> *A vivid and sudden feeling of admiration, of surprise, which one feels in seeing, hearing, knowing something that is or appears to be new, extraordinary, strange or otherwise unexpected.*

Although in the common imagination, the concept of wonder has a positive value, the dictionary does not give too many precise indications on the matter, it is specified that this feeling comes from extraordinary, strange and unexpected things.

What is strange, always from the dictionary, is

different from the usual or the common, from the normal, very singular, so as to arouse wonder, amazement, curiosity

while if the adjective refers to a person:

referring to a person, who has a character, a way of thinking and feeling and generally a behaviour different from that of most men; said especially of those who are rather closed in on themselves, more inclined to think and fantasize than to talk.

There is no doubt that Caravaggio was a strange person and that he dedicated himself to the creation of strange works. Our Michelangelo Merisi is an artist who was able (and still knows today) to create wonder with his works.

The theme of amazement and wonder brings us to an age-old problem that disturbs the sleepless nights of Art critics and lovers: what are the limits that must be respected in the search for amazement?

Before going into the discussion, it is good to clarify two aspects that are too often confused in the artistic field (and to reflect well in life too): *ethics* and *morality*.

Let us expand on a theme that we have already touched upon a few chapters ago.

Ethics is a real doctrine that investigates the practical behaviour of man in the face of the two basic concepts of existence which are good and evil. The Greek origin of the word brings us the meanings of "behaviour", "character" and "custom".

Morality, on the other hand, is a free choice of the individual or the community regarding one's behaviour. Moral choices usually originate mainly from social and political reality, obviously they also refer to the set of traditions of the individual or the society to which he belongs.

While ethics has a more universal value and survives time and changes in societies and traditions, morality can vary with the changing social reality and political ideas.

Ethics does not require a real effort of understanding, precisely because it is a value that is not subject to variation; instead, to understand morality it is necessary to know the social and political reality and consequently an effort must be made to move away from our current morality to embrace (even if temporarily) that of the time that aroused our interest.

Now, thanks to this minimal and superficial clarification regarding these two important aspects of human life and knowledge, let us put everything aside and forget about various ethics and morals. Art should not be interested and harnessed by any of these aspects, and Caravaggio did not let himself be easily harnessed.

Wonder also passes through the scandal. We have already seen how Caravaggio enjoyed giving scandal with the choice of models and settings.

Today, as then, Art is always engaged in the search for scandal. To put it in all sincerity, Art must give scandal to allow us to think outside the normal thinking and, even more important and essential, to question our certainties.

An ethical and moral Art cannot exist, because it would not be faithful to its truest essence and would turn into mere propaganda. In a utopian world, morality should only concern politics and society while religion should only be interested in ethics; we do not live in a utopia, unfortunately, and often religion has dedicated itself even to morality.

Respecting the politically correct in Art and not having to contravene ethical and moral rules distort Art to such an extent as to make it window dressing: the sublime Art of presenting a product (which can also be an ideal) making it a necessity for those who are captivated by the aesthetic beauty of the showcase prepared on purpose to grab our attention.

Art can devote itself to scandal in order to offer a different starting point of thought but also for pure and simple fun.

How beautiful it is sometimes to create reactions of amazement in others and to see the consequences of our being provocative. Not so much for the discomfort that can be noticed in our interlocutors but for the possibility that is unleashed (at times) to be able to discuss and broaden one's vision.

We should guarantee a free zone to artists, where they are allowed to do everything, without restrictions or limitations. There should be no judgments or censures for having damaged the decorum of some ideology or to highlight its weaker sides.

What should be severely punished, without a shadow of a doubt, is the social behaviour that incites violence (verbal and physical) as well as the disrespect for the ideas of others.

We cannot ask Art to take on an educational or training task. It is not up to it to train people, much less to offer a channel to access culture. What Art must do, however, is to stimulate the public's thinking and sensitivity.

All the strong and established powers (from political to religious) have exploited the evocative power of Art, making it the privileged channel of propaganda and indoctrination. For too long we have asked Art to tell us stories, when instead we should have asked it to help us reflect and think.

In more remote times, the involvement of Art also served to overcome the limits that were created due to the high level of illiteracy. Today, however, despite the relapse into illiteracy is very high and decidedly worrying, Art should be free from this social commitment (which is sometimes also a pure and simple pretext) and devote itself to its true mission: to see beyond.

Today, still too often, we happen to witness unfortunate episodes of censorship. Prohibiting artistic expression because it is irreverent is a real crime.

Even Michelangelo Merisi did not want to completely yield to this respectable trend that would like a more educated and less scandalous Art. We have seen works and read poems born of his genius that were downright outrageous; today, however, perhaps due to the ever-increasing distance in time, we are less intransigent towards him. His contemporaries were, however, very disturbed by his provocations, so much so that they came to withdraw works and reject them. Today, the faces of prostitutes for us have become mere faces of women and we no longer experience outrage. By the way, we can imagine the wonder of the time in having to accept these choices of the artist.

Crying out scandal is the shortest and easiest way not to question oneself. One of the many phrases attributed to Oscar Wilde (hoping it is real) says:

> *Gossip is charming! History is merely gossip. But scandal is gossip made tedious by morality.*

It is with full knowledge of the facts that one can safely hope in the proliferation of scandals in Art; the most intense and direct way so that we can be impressed, reflect and maybe we can find comfort and solution among the many doubts that can haunt us in daily life.

Scene V:
The goose that lays the golden eggs

As we have seen previously, Michelangelo Merisi never wanted to open his own workshop, much less surround himself with pupils.

Bernard Berenson was a prominent American Art critic and more than anyone else stated with great clarity that

> with the exception of Michelangelo [30], no other Italian painter exerted such a great influence on later painters.

An important aspect is that of the influence that has led many artists to follow in Caravaggio's footsteps. As we have seen, many painters have taken inspiration from his painting technique, developing in turn an artistic path and language.

Unfortunately, the fame of the Lombard master has reached such a high level of public appreciation that it has become very popular on the market. Even the fastest artistic production could not satisfy all the requests of the general public and when this happens we usually turn to copies, which have a lower commercial value and are available in more copies. Today we would resort to lithographs and prints (of excellent workmanship or cheap), at the time of Caravaggio to be the most popular were the good author counterfeiters (cheap but of great effect).

Caravaggio has always been very rigid towards his fellow painters:

> *Li valent'huomini sono quelli che si intendono della pittura et giudicaranno buoni pittori quelli che ho giudicato io buoni et cattivi; ma quelli che sono cattivi*

---

[30] Berenson obviously refers to Michelangelo Merisi.

> *pittori et ignoranti giudicaranno per buoni pittori*
> *gl'ignoranti come sono loro³¹.*

It would now be necessary to understand what were the canons to judge positively or negatively the other painters and also in this case we can once again rely on the words of the Milanese master:

> *La parola valent'huomo appresso di me vuol dire che sappi far bene, cioè sappi far bene dell'arte sua, così in pittura valent'huomo che sappi dipingere bene et imitar bene le cose naturali³².*

It is easy to understand Merisi's words: those who make Art using Nature as a model are good, those who use other things (the works of other painters, for example) are not.

And here one would ask: all those who have created their career by making copies of existing works, how would they be considered by Caravaggio?

---

[31] Valiant men are those who knows about painting and those whom I have judged good and bad; but those who are bad painters and ignorant will judge those ignorant as they are good painters.

[32] The word, talented man, for me means that you know how to do well, that is, you know how to do well of your art, so a talented painter, who knows how to paint well and imitate natural things well

If we consider that the artist is the one who has to create a fracture in the unfolding of History (he should be like those enormously heavy masses of the universe that manage to divert the path of any energy and object that passes near them), we can understand quite easily which is the responsibility of the true artist and how much his work is worth.

Often, however, whoever presents himself as an artist is nothing more than a person without skills.

If Art is one of the most sublime expressions of mankind, simply copying the works of others should never be considered "making Art". This obviously should be applied to all artistic expressions; you can be inspired, you can also revisit a painting, a song or a statue but simply copying without putting some of your own point of view and thinking is demeaning.

To be honest, Caravaggio's Art is an invitation to copy and settle on his ideas, because today (more than ever, to tell the truth) it sells very well.

We are finally ready to understand his poetics and aesthetics and everything that is presented under his aegis is much appreciated.

For many Michelangelo Merisi represents an easy entry into the Art market, sometimes it is enough to simply copy one of his paintings to be considered artists.

But as we know, an artist should shine with his own light, not the reflected one. This continuous revival without character, if we really have to be honest, is also the fault of an audience that wants to remain in the comfort zone of the already seen and already understood. We know very well that the novelty is not only difficult to understand but sometimes you do not have the right mental openness to understand them; at least not immediately.

It would be really curious to know what Caravaggio would think of all those "serial copiers" that are present on the market. Knowing his thought and the colourful language he used in these cases, I think he would have enjoyed it, and not a little.

Today his brand is selling, but this is a relatively recent situation compared to what he really deserved.

One wish is to see this path traced by the great Milanese master flourish but in an intelligent way. We all know the old popular adage that one must always try to surpass the teacher; unfortunately, we must be honest and not hide that this is the prerogative only of those students who have a considerable value; the mediocre just copy.

Today the Arts are facing a crossroads: nostalgia as an end in itself or nostalgic overcoming? Those with poor skills and abilities limit themselves to a nostalgic copy of the past that at the beginning of a career can also bring a certain economic benefit (since it is judged by an audience that always needs to be reassured with the nostalgia of the past) but then inexorably drops into the abyss of oblivion. This is what happened to those who copied in the past and, unfortunately for them, it will happen to all serial copiers of today.

Those who, on the other hand, embark on a path of in-depth research of the artists of the past, can fully collect the aesthetics and seeds of ideas left by the great masters of the past, which offer new strength to the life of Art.

Obviously, inventing from scratch in the world of Art is quite impossible, every expression and every true work are based on humanity and on History and express doubts, joys and pains of the time we are living in. Today the Arts are returning to the classic, virtuous and beautiful lines but they are not cold and perfect as Canova wanted them.

The new Art is made of flesh and blood. We see more and more works made with sublime techniques impregnated with strong emotions.

Caravaggio was a precursor of this way of doing Art and, today, we are not only reaping the copious fruits but we are witnessing a new evolution of the artistic language, which promises great strong and contrasting emotions.

Finally, Caravaggio is living among his contemporaries and is in dialogue with artists who can understand him.

Someone will get some nice-coloured reproaches, because they will limit themselves to exploiting the good name of Michelangelo Merisi to make money and make a name for themselves without having to be too innovative, someone else will instead receive compliments and will be remembered for the new language that started from one of the greatest masters that the history of Italian Art has ever had.

To be a true artist it is essential to be honest with yourself, to get naked in your work and to offer the world your own vision of reality, nothing more complicated.

CURTAIN

PROSCENIUM	**5**
ACT ONE	**7**
SCENE I: LADIES AND GENTLEMEN, THE DIRECTOR	9
SCENE II: THE MYSTERY OF A NAME	13
SCENE III: AN ARTIST WITH A STRONG CHARACTER	19
SCENE IV: ON THE EDGE OF THE CENTRE OF SOCIETY	27
SCENE V: A LONG TRAIL OF VIOLENCE	33
SCENE VI: A LIFE ON THE RUN	43
SCENE VII: THE THEATRICAL DIRECTION	47
SCENE VIII: THE DAUBER	55
SCENE IX: DEAD MAN WALKING!	63
SCENE X: LIKE OSCAR	77
ACT TWO	**83**
SCENE I: THE LIGHT THAT CREATES	85
SCENE II: MASTERFUL BLACK	91
SCENE III: THE BEGGARS	97
SCENE IV: THAT VIRGIN THAT EVERYONE KNEW	103
SCENE V: A LITTLE BIT OF GOSSIP	111
SCENE VI: SQUARING THE CIRCLE	121
SCENE VII: THE INFLUENCE OF POWER	127
SCENE VIII: THE ORDER OF CARAVAGGIO	133
BACKSTAGE	**145**
SCENE I: THE DESIGNER	147
SCENE II: THE ART OF CAPRICCIO	153
SCENE III: THE INFLUENCE OF BORROMEO	159
SCENE IV: SCANDAL!	167
SCENE V: THE GOOSE THAT LAYS THE GOLDEN EGGS	175

www.ingramcontent.com/pod-product-compliance
Lightning Source LLC
Chambersburg PA
CBHW030632220526
45463CB00004B/1492